Workbook

Principles of Human Services

by

Michelle McCoy
Family and Consumer Sciences Instructor
Hendrickson High School
Pflugerville, Texas

Publisher
The Goodheart-Willcox Company, Inc.
Tinley Park, IL
www.g-w.com

Copyright © 2018
by
The Goodheart-Willcox Company, Inc.

All rights reserved. No part of this work may be reproduced, stored, or transmitted in any form or by any electronic or mechanical means, including information storage and retrieval systems, without the prior written permission of The Goodheart-Willcox Company, Inc.

Manufactured in the United States of America.

ISBN: 978-1-63126-535-8

1 2 3 4 5 6 7 8 9 – 18 – 22 21 20 19 18 17 16

The Goodheart-Willcox Company, Inc. Brand Disclaimer: Brand names, company names, and illustrations for products and services included in this text are provided for educational purposes only and do not represent or imply endorsement or recommendation by the author or the publisher.

The Goodheart-Willcox Company, Inc. Safety Notice: The reader is expressly advised to carefully read, understand, and apply all safety precautions and warnings described in this book or that might also be indicated in undertaking the activities and exercises described herein to minimize risk of personal injury or injury to others. Common sense and good judgment should also be exercised and applied to help avoid all potential hazards. The reader should always refer to the appropriate manufacturer's technical information, directions, and recommendations; then proceed with care to follow specific equipment operating instructions. The reader should understand these notices and cautions are not exhaustive.

The publisher makes no warranty or representation whatsoever, either expressed or implied, including but not limited to equipment, procedures, and applications described or referred to herein, their quality, performance, merchantability, or fitness for a particular purpose. The publisher assumes no responsibility for any changes, errors, or omissions in this book. The publisher specifically disclaims any liability whatsoever, including any direct, indirect, incidental, consequential, special, or exemplary damages resulting, in whole or in part, from the reader's use or reliance upon the information, instructions, procedures, warnings, cautions, applications, or other matter contained in this book. The publisher assumes no responsibility for the activities of the reader.

The Goodheart-Willcox Company, Inc. Internet Disclaimer: The Internet resources and listings in this Goodheart-Willcox Publisher product are provided solely as a convenience to you. These resources and listings were reviewed at the time of publication to provide you with accurate, safe, and appropriate information. Goodheart-Willcox Publisher has no control over the referenced websites and, due to the dynamic nature of the Internet, is not responsible or liable for the content, products, or performance of links to other websites or resources. Goodheart-Willcox Publisher makes no representation, either expressed or implied, regarding the content of these websites, and such references do not constitute an endorsement or recommendation of the information or content presented. It is your responsibility to take all protective measures to guard against inappropriate content, viruses, or other destructive elements.

Front cover images (clockwise from left with classroom being the farthest left): michaeljung/Shutterstock.com, ©iStock.com/omgimages, wavebreakmedia/Shutterstock.com, bikeriderlondon/Shutterstock.com, Monkey Business Images/Shutterstock.com

Back cover images (clockwise): ©iStock.com/digitalskillet, antoniodiaz/Shutterstock.com, ©iStock.com/perkmeup

Contents

Unit 1 Learning About Human Services

Chapter 1 An Introduction to Human Services 7
- Activity A   Development of the Human Services Career Field 7
- Activity B   Employment Categories in Human Services 8
- Activity C   Common Characteristics of Human Services Workers 9
- Activity D   Portability Skills 10
- Activity E   Education and Training Terms 11
- Activity F   Meeting Professional Qualifications 12

Chapter 2 The People Business 13
- Activity A   Theories and Theorists of Human Development 13
- Activity B   Growth and Development Time Line 15
- Activity C   Maslow's Hierarchy of Human Needs 16
- Activity D   Identifying Resources 17
- Activity E   Compare the Cost of Living 18
- Activity F   Comparing Food Purchasing Assistance Programs 19

Chapter 3 What Makes an Effective Human Services Worker? 21
- Activity A   Communication 101 21
- Activity B   Clues to Body Language 22
- Activity C   Communication Mix-Up 23
- Activity D   Decision-Making Skills 25
- Activity E   Self-Assessment of Leadership Skills 27
- Activity F   Identifying Leaders 29

Chapter 4 On the Road to Personal and Professional Success 31
- Activity A   Good Grooming 31
- Activity B   Healthy or Hazardous? 32
- Activity C   Ethics in the Workplace 33
- Activity D   Professional Organization Research 35
- Activity E   Can You Manage Your Time Wisely? 36
- Activity F   Rate Your Stress 37

Unit 2 Preparing for Career Success

Chapter 5 Looking Inward: Identifying Your Personal Brand 39
- Activity A   Graffiti Wall Activity 39
- Activity B   Interpersonal Skills Inventory 40

Activity C	Celebrating Personal Accomplishments	41
Activity D	Who Is Your Mentor?	42
Activity E	What Would You Do?	43
Activity F	Setting My Goals	45

Chapter 6 Looking Outward: Connecting with Human Services 47
Activity A	Gaining Firsthand Knowledge	47
Activity B	Understanding the *Occupational Outlook Handbook*	48
Activity C	Researching with the *Occupational Outlook Handbook*	49
Activity D	Choosing Classes in School	51
Activity E	Comparing College Costs	53
Activity F	Student Organization Internet Quest	54

Chapter 7 Looking Ahead: Preparing for Workplace Success 55
Activity A	Investigating Job Openings	55
Activity B	Completing an Application	56
Activity C	Writing a Résumé	57
Activity D	What Is in a Cover Message?	59
Activity E	Personal Portfolios	60
Activity F	Starting a New Job	61

Unit 3 Investigating Career Pathways in Human Services

Chapter 8 Consumer Services 63
Activity A	Careers in Consumer Services	63
Activity B	Consumer Rights and Responsibilities	64
Activity C	Evaluating Advertising Claims	65
Activity D	Writing a Letter of Complaint	66
Activity E	Practicing Customer Service	67
Activity F	Consumer Services Terms	69

Chapter 9 Counseling and Mental Health Services 71
Activity A	An Informational Interview	71
Activity B	Individual and Family Life Cycle	74
Activity C	Coping with Family-Life Crises	75
Activity D	Preparing for Death	77
Activity E	Identifying the Stages of Grieving	78
Activity F	Counseling and Mental Health Terms	79

Chapter 10 Early Childhood Development and Services 81
Activity A	Child Care Match Up	81
Activity B	Interviewing a Child Caregiver	82
Activity C	Developmental Milestones	85

Activity D	Discipline and Parenting Styles	86
Activity E	Creating a Safe Environment	87
Activity F	Identifying Child Abuse	88

Chapter 11   Family and Community Services 89

Activity A	Exploring Careers in Family and Community Services	89
Activity B	Family Structures	90
Activity C	Functions of the Family	91
Activity D	Finding Community Resources	92
Activity E	Public Policy and Families	93
Activity F	Volunteer Hours Sheet	96

Chapter 12   Personal Care Services 97

Activity A	An Informational Interview	97
Activity B	Helping Hands	100
Activity C	Writing Obituaries	101
Activity D	Cosmetology License Requirements	103
Activity E	Client Records	104
Activity F	Using Technology to Promote Personal Care Services	105
Activity G	Understanding Changes in Older Adulthood	106

Unit 4   Exploring Human Services Related Careers

Chapter 13   Entrepreneurial Careers in Human Services 107

Activity A	Defining Entrepreneurship	107
Activity B	Statements About Entrepreneurs	109
Activity C	Star Abilities	110
Activity D	SWOT Analysis of a Business	111
Activity E	Ownership Advantages and Disadvantages	112
Activity F	Parts of a Business Plan	113

Chapter 14   Food and Nutrition Related Human Services 115

Activity A	Career Match Up	115
Activity B	Establishing a Healthy Eating Style	116
Activity C	Comparing Nutritional Needs	119
Activity D	Fad Diets—Myth or Truth?	121
Activity E	Understanding Recipes	123

Chapter 15   Clothing Related Human Services 125

Activity A	An Informational Interview	125
Activity B	Fashion Forecast—Trend or Bust?	128
Activity C	Clothing Needs Across the Life Cycle	129
Activity D	Laundry Signs Identification	130

Activity E   Identifying Construction Tools 131
  Activity F   Making Simple Repairs and Alterations.. 133

Chapter 16 Housing Related Human Services 135
  Activity A   Housing Related Career Research... 135
  Activity B   An Informational Interview 136
  Activity C   Changing Housing Needs 139
  Activity D   Understanding Universal Design.. 140
  Activity E   Creating a Cleaning and Maintenance Schedule 141
  Activity F   Using the Elements of Design 142
  Activity G   The Principles of Design 143
  Activity H   Housing Related Terms Review 144

Chapter 1: An Introduction to Human Services

Development of the Human Services Career Field

Activity A
Chapter 1

Name _____
Date _____ Period _____

Human services is a relatively new career field that has only been around for the past 100 years or so. During this time, many events have changed the way people think about who is responsible to meet needs and how to meet them. For this activity, read the following descriptions about events in history. Then identify which time frame or person brought about the improvement.

Events in History

_____ 1. Group homes were built to care for older adults with no family.

_____ 2. An act of legislation that provided for the retired elderly and widows and dependent children of deceased workers.

_____ 3. Urban density became an issue.

_____ 4. Enacted legislation that focused on offering relief for those in need and recovery from crisis.

_____ 5. Began the Charitable Organization Society (COS).

_____ 6. Career opportunities in the human services field expanded at a rapid pace.

_____ 7. Founded the US Settlement House Movement.

_____ 8. Programs like Head Start and the Family Medical Leave Act were implemented.

_____ 9. New programs continue to be developed to meet people's needs.

_____ 10. Shift in thought began to occur as families came together in urban areas.

Person or Time Frame of Interest

A. after the Great Depression
B. beginning of the twentieth century
C. Industrial Revolution
D. Jane Addams
E. Jean Piaget
F. later part of the twentieth century
G. Lev Vygotsky
H. Mary Richmond
I. President Franklin D. Roosevelt
J. Social Security Act of 1935

Employment Categories in Human Services

Activity B Name _____

Chapter 1 Date _____ Period _____

Depending on your education and career goals, there are a range of human services careers from which you can choose. Most human services careers fall under one or more of the broad employment categories shown in the left-hand column of the table below.

Complete the table by filling in the middle column with descriptions showcasing the types of services workers provide within these categories. In the right-hand column, list three examples of careers within each of the employment categories.

Broad Employment Categories	Descriptions	Examples of Careers
Consumer services		
Counseling and mental health services		
Early childhood development and services		
Family and community services		
Personal care services		
Entrepreneurial careers		
Related services in food		
Related services in clothing		
Related services in housing		

Common Characteristics of Human Services Workers

Activity C
Chapter 1

Name _____

Date _____ Period _____

Human services workers share common characteristics that help them excel at their chosen professions. In the left-hand column of the following table, list some common characteristics that human services workers exhibit. In the right-hand column, list your personal characteristics that would help in a career as a human services worker.

Characteristics of Human Services Workers	My Characteristics

Portability Skills

Activity D
Chapter 1

Name _____

Date _____ Period _____

Complete this chart with personal facts and skills that apply to you. When you are finished, you will have information to help you prepare a portability skills list.

Volunteer Activities	**Hobbies**

Sports	**Life Experiences**

School

Education and Training Terms

Activity E
Chapter 1

Name _____

Date _____ Period _____

Students in human services learn knowledge and practical skills that prepare them to help people and meet their needs. Using the terms listed below, fill in the blanks in the statements that follow.

Terms		
allocate	community college	Industrial Revolution interdisciplinary
apprenticeship	competencies	master's degree
associate's degree	doctorate degree	on-the-job training
bachelor's degree	high school	paraprofessionals
career and technical program	ideology	portable
certifications	impoverished	postsecondary
college		

A (1)_____ is a course of study that prepares students for careers in specific trades and occupations that need skilled workers. These programs combine academics and job-specific skills, and are available for (2)_____ and (3)_____ students.

An (4)_____ involves working for a qualified professional to learn a skilled trade. Workers earn a salary while learning important skills they need to succeed in a high-demand career. These vary in how long they last. Some may last for a year while others can last four years.

(5)_____ educational requirements vary by occupation or specific career field. A four-year degree is commonly needed for many jobs today. Human services occupations often require experience, too. Many human services careers provide (6)_____ so workers can learn about the specific job duties and responsibilities.

When preparing for careers in human services, educational requirements may include an (7)_____, or two-year degree earned through a (8)_____. A (9)_____, or four-year degree, is earned through colleges and universities. Advanced degrees include a (10)_____ and a (11)_____, which is the highest degree a person can earn.

In addition to a degree, some human services careers also require state licensure, (12)_____, or professional registration. Sometimes these additional requirements are earned through hours in practice, a qualifying exam, or a combination of both.

Meeting Professional Qualifications

Activity F
Chapter 1

Name _____

Date _____ Period _____

Studying and training are needed to obtain the knowledge and skills necessary for successful careers in the field of human services. Find written information or interview a person concerning the needed professional qualifications for a human services career that interests you. Then provide the information requested below.

1. Name of career in a human services related field: _____

2. List the preprofessional preparation needed (any preparation needed before being allowed to study or train in a given field).

   _____
   _____
   _____
   _____
   _____
   _____
   _____

3. What is the nature and length of the professional study or training required? _____

   _____
   _____
   _____
   _____
   _____
   _____

4. Describe specialization(s) within the profession. What additional professional preparation is needed for the specialization(s)?

   _____
   _____
   _____
   _____
   _____
   _____
   _____

Chapter 2 The People Business

Theories and Theorists of Human Development

Activity A
Chapter 2

Name _____

Date _____ Period _____

Researchers and scientists explore the many ways in which humans grow and develop. As a result of observation and experiments, they have drawn conclusions based on their studies and earlier studies by others. For this activity, match each statement to its proper theory or theorist. (As you study the textbook, you will read similar statements again.)

Statements About Theories

_____ 1. People are affected by rewards and punishments, but their reactions to them are filtered by their own perceptions, thoughts, and motivations.

_____ 2. Ideas about how people process information, think, and learn.

_____ 3. Analyze the symbolic meaning behind behaviors.

_____ 4. Repetition of behaviors when reinforced.

_____ 5. Belief that people's behavior is determined by forces in the environment that are beyond their control.

_____ 6. Comprehensive explanations about why people act and behave the way they do and how they change over time.

_____ 7. Behaviors associated with emotional responses.

_____ 8. Belief that much development happens at an unconscious level and is buried in emotions.

_____ 9. Belief that to make a behavior stick, the reinforcement must be gradually removed following an unpredictable pattern.

_____ 10. People must successfully resolve a psychological and/or social conflict. If they do not, their failure to do so will affect future stages of development.

_____ 11. As children gain more experience, their way of thinking will change and adapt.

_____ 12. Belief that a child who observes a kind act may later imitate the same act toward a sibling or classmate.

Theories

A. behaviorism
B. classical conditioning
C. cognitive theory
D. developmental theories
E. operant conditioning
F. psychoanalytic theories
G. social cognitive theory

(Continued)

Statements About Theorists

Theorists

A. Bandura
B. Erikson
C. Freud
D. Gilligan
E. Kohlberg
F. Pavlov
G. Piaget
H. Skinner
I. Vygotsky

_____ 1. Theorist who believed that what happens early in life affects a person for years to come.

_____ 2. Theorized that the social and cultural environment shapes human cognitive development.

_____ 3. Believed how a person responds is based on personal reaction and how he or she processes information.

_____ 4. Recognized that children do not think like adults.

_____ 5. Identified three levels of thinking that people go through in making moral decisions.

_____ 6. Theorist who used repetition of behavior with reinforcement gradually being removed.

_____ 7. Theorized that all humans develop through experimentation with objects.

_____ 8. Explains how children are active in their own development and learning.

_____ 9. Expanded on Kohlberg's theory by considering how women and girls make moral decisions.

_____ 10. Theorist who believed that development is a social process.

_____ 11. Demonstrated his theory using a dog.

_____ 12. Argued that people are very different from Pavlov's dog, and are much more complex.

_____ 13. Described the stages of cognitive development in four stages.

_____ 14. Believed that personality can develop in ways that are healthy or unhealthy.

_____ 15. Pioneer in applying psychoanalytic theory.

_____ 16. Theorized that all humans develop in eight psychosocial development stages.

Growth and Development Time Line

Activity B
Chapter 2

Name _____

Date _____ Period _____

Human services workers benefit from understanding several approaches to development and being able to apply them to clients of all ages. Using the following theories, as well as the various stages in each theory, create a time line from birth to death by filling in the following table. If a theory falls under more than one age, be sure to note that as well. A sample entry is completed for you.

Theories

Erikson's Psychosocial Theory
Piaget's Cognitive Theory
Kohlberg's Theory of Moral Development

Birth → **Time Line** → **Death**

Birth	**Birth to 1 year** Erikson's Psychosocial Theory—trust versus mistrust **Birth to 2 years** Piaget's Cognitive Theory—sensorimotor
Childhood	
Adolescence	
Adulthood	

Maslow's Hierarchy of Human Needs

Activity C

Chapter 2

Name _____

Date _____ Period _____

Human psychologist Abraham Maslow theorized that all people have the same basic needs to survive. He believed you had to meet the needs of each level before moving on to another level. Identify and describe each level of needs in Maslow's *Hierarchy of Human Needs*, beginning with Level 1.

```
        5
       4
      3
     2
    1
```

Level 1: _____
_____
_____

Level 2: _____
_____
_____

Level 3: _____
_____
_____

Level 4: _____
_____
_____

Level 5: _____
_____
_____

Identifying Resources

Activity D
Chapter 2

Name _____

Date _____ Period _____

Unscramble the letters to identify terms related to resources. Then, give an example of each type and how to use the resource.

1. TINYMOCMU RECERSSOU _____
_____
_____

2. MUHNA RECERSSOU _____
_____
_____

3. RATLANU RECERSSOU _____
_____
_____

4. TIERALMA RECERSSOU _____
_____
_____

5. WORKCORE _____
_____
_____

6. MITE _____
_____
_____

7. NOYEM _____
_____
_____

8. PIEQUENTM _____
_____
_____

9. RGYNEE _____
_____
_____

10. OODF _____
_____
_____

Compare the Cost of Living

Activity E
Chapter 2

Name _____

Date _____ Period _____

Use the following table to compare the cost of living for two different cities in your area. Then answer the questions.

Comparison Items	Cost in City #1	Cost in City #2
Cost of a home		
Apartment rent		
Tire balance		
Vet services		
Beauty salon		
Women's slacks		
Men's shirt		
Boy's jeans		
Haircut		
T-bone steak		
Dry cleaning		
Ground beef (1 pound)		
Coffee		
Hamburger		
Two pieces chicken		
Potato chips		
Bowling		
Orange juice		
Dozen eggs		
Gallon of milk		
Gallon of gasoline		
Mortgage rate		

1. Which town would be cheaper to live in? _____

2. What factors are you basing that decision on? _____

_____

_____

Comparing Food Purchasing Assistance Programs

Activity F
Chapter 2

Name _____
Date _____ Period _____

When the economy is in a recession mode, there is a slowing and decline in the economy. During this time, more people access food banks and subsidized government programs to help them meet their needs. For this activity, identify which of the following food purchasing assistance programs are available in your area. Choose one of the programs to research and respond to the following questions. Share your findings with the rest of the class.

Food Purchasing Assistance Programs
• Supplemental Nutritional Assistance Program (SNAP)—Formerly known as *Food Stamps* • Special Supplemental Program for Women, Infants, and Children (WIC) • Commodity Supplemental Food Program (CSFP) • WIC and Senior Farmers' Market Nutrition Program (FMNP)

1. Which of these programs are available in my area? _____

_____

2. Which program am I researching? _____

3. What criteria must a person meet to be eligible to receive services from this program? _____

_____

4. Does the program cost a user any money? If so, how much? _____

(Continued)

5. Where would I have to go to receive these services? _____
_____
_____

6. For how long can I receive these services? _____
_____
_____

7. Who operates this program in my town? _____
_____

8. Under what conditions can the aid I am receiving be taken away? _____
_____
_____
_____
_____
_____
_____

9. Are there any actions I am prohibited from doing while on this program? If so, what are they?
_____
_____
_____
_____
_____
_____
_____

10. How often a month can I receive services from this program? _____
_____

Chapter 3: What Makes an Effective Human Services Worker?

Communication 101

Activity A
Chapter 3

Name _____

Date _____ Period _____

In any job you have, you will be expected to communicate with people. Sometimes you may only need to communicate with one person while other times you may need to communicate with multiple people. In this activity, match the types of communication with the statements about communication.

Statements About Communication

_____ 1. Aisha writes an e-mail to her coworker.

_____ 2. Marcel asks his boss a question.

_____ 3. Rosa shrugs her shoulders in response to a question asked of her.

_____ 4. Gabrielle writes a letter to her grandmother.

_____ 5. Sarah crooks her finger at her little sister.

_____ 6. Zahra leaves a note on her front door for the mailman.

_____ 7. Rashid posts an update on a social media site.

_____ 8. Kyle sings a song to his daughter.

_____ 9. Liam winks at Emily.

_____ 10. Janet stomps her foot at her little brother.

_____ 11. Peter reads a book.

_____ 12. Sheng posts a video on a social media site.

_____ 13. Elena and Juan have an argument.

_____ 14. Katie calls Tatiana on her cell phone.

_____ 15. Rhonda sends an instant message to her brother.

_____ 16. John rolls his eyes at his mother's request to take out the garbage.

_____ 17. Toby asks Alexandra to the prom.

_____ 18. Kamal leads a group discussion in class.

_____ 19. Lin smiles at her best friend.

_____ 20. Tanesha completes her college application.

Types of Communication

A. electronic communication

B. nonverbal communication

C. verbal communication

D. written communication

Clues to Body Language

Activity B
Chapter 3

Name _____
Date _____ Period _____

For each example of body language in the table below, describe one possible meaning and write it in the space provided. Then answer the questions that follow.

Examples of Body Language	Possible Meanings
1. Biting fingernails	
2. Smiling	
3. Tapping fingers or a pencil	
4. Gazing into the distance	
5. Shrugging shoulders	
6. Rolling the eyes	
7. Twisting hair or fingering jewelry	
8. Chewing gum vigorously	
9. Nodding	
10. Shaping hand limply	
11. Slouching in a chair	
12. Smirking	
13. Frowning	
14. Shaking head *no*	

15. Is body language always a clue to what someone is feeling? Explain. _____
_____
_____
_____

16. How does body language affect communication? _____
_____
_____

Communication Mix-Up

Activity C
Chapter 3

Name _____

Date _____ Period _____

Do you listen and hear? Unscramble the basics of good communication in the following sentences and write your answers in the spaces provided.

1. Words are not used in BARNLOVEN communication.

    _____

2. Two-way communication means you must EVERICE messages as well as send them.

    _____

3. Your LAACFI NIXPSEERSOS may negate any verbal comments you make.

    _____

4. If you want to communicate, remove CANDOTSISTIR, such as the radio and television.

    _____

5. If you do not control your SOONTIME, you may miss what someone is saying to you.

    _____

6. Unlike GINHARE, listening requires concentrating, understanding, and remembering.

    _____

7. Making YEE TANCCOT means looking directly at someone.

    _____

8. Your NASMERN are the way you behave toward other people.

    _____

9. The image you have of someone you just met is your NOSIPERMIS.

    _____

10. To establish meaningful relationships, incorporate SHENTOY in your communication.

    _____

11. Your words may have different messages, depending on your NOTE FO OCEVI.

    _____

12. If you are SITIPOVE about listening, you act as if you expect to hear something.

    _____

13. PISGOS is a negative form of communication.

    _____

(Continued)

14. Good IMORGONG means having a clean and healthy appearance.
    _____

15. Standing tall, or having good USERPOT, shows that you feel good about yourself.
    _____

16. Mutual CEPTSRE is important for two-way communication.
    _____

17. You need to CRITPACE listening to build skills in concentrating, understanding, and remembering.
    _____

18. By giving DEFBAECK, you let someone know you are listening.
    _____

19. Effective speaking requires ROILINGAT your message to a particular audience or client.
    _____

20. Thinking about what you say FROBEE speaking is very important.
    _____

21. Messages that are YECLALR communicated are less likely to be misunderstood.
    _____

22. RAIVSEETS communicators send straightforward messages.
    _____

23. To show THEMPAY is to identify with and share another person's feelings.
    _____

24. RUNGINTPERTI someone while he or she is still speaking is a sign that you are not listening.
    _____

25. Sending EXMID SEASGEMS can cause communication to break down.
    _____

Decision-Making Skills

Activity D
Chapter 3

Name _____

Date _____ Period _____

Everyone makes decisions on a daily basis. Whether those decisions are simple or complex differs based on the type of decision to be made. Read the following scenarios and make a decision on what to do in the situation. Explain your reasoning for making this decision, and indicate whether you thought this decision was simple or difficult to make.

Scenario 1 *You get invited to a party that most of your friends are also invited to, but not your best friend, who was left out on purpose. What would you do?*

My decision: _____

_____

Why I made this decision: _____

_____

_____

_____

Was this decision simple or difficult to make? _____

Scenario 2 *You have a huge incomplete project due Monday, and your cousin who is only in town for five days has asked you to go camping all weekend. You currently have a D in the class. What would you do?*

My decision: _____

_____

Why I made this decision: _____

_____

_____

_____

Was this decision simple or difficult to make? _____

Scenario 3 *You received a bad grade in class and have to bring home a letter from your teacher, which needs to be signed by a parent. You think about forging your parent's signature. What would you do?*

My decision: _____

_____

Why I made this decision: _____

_____

_____

_____

Was this decision simple or difficult to make? _____

(Continued)

Scenario 4 *You are a freshman and an only child whose parents have demanding careers and little time to spend at home. You are left home alone a lot and have friends over for parties all the time. The parties occasionally get out of hand, but you have not been caught. Recently, your friends have challenged you to take them for a ride in your parent's car. You don't have your license yet. What do you do?*

My decision: _____

_____

Why I made this decision: _____

_____

_____

_____

Was this decision simple or difficult to make? _____

Scenario 5 *A not-so-popular student has invited you to a sleepover at a birthday party on Friday night. You have accepted the invitation and are planning to attend. On Wednesday, you are invited to a party for the same Friday night by one of the most popular students in your school, someone you have hoped to become friends with. After talking with your friends, you realize most of them are planning to attend the popular student's party. Your parents have told you it's your decision, but that you should attend the party you respond to first. You really want to be a part of the popular crowd. What do you do?*

My decision: _____

_____

Why I made this decision: _____

_____

_____

_____

Was this decision simple or difficult to make? _____

Scenario 6 *You are sitting with your two best friends, Michael and Mya, at lunch. Michael leaves to throw away some trash and Mya starts to tell you a story about Michael. The story sounds like gossip to hurt Michael's reputation. What do you do?*

My decision: _____

_____

Why I made this decision: _____

_____

_____

_____

Was this decision simple or difficult to make? _____

Self-Assessment of Leadership Skills

Activity E
Chapter 3

Name _____

Date _____ Period _____

This self-assessment is designed to help you determine which leadership skills you may need to develop. Please read each statement carefully. Then use the rating scale provided to rate yourself in terms of how well you think you possess the attribute or perform the leadership skill. Review your personal rating responses and then complete the statements at the end of the activity.

Rating Scale
1 = I do not possess this attribute or do this skill well at all.
2 = I seldom possess this attribute or do this skill somewhat well.
3 = I possess this attribute or do this skill very well.

_____ 1. I articulate my vision and mission to others.

_____ 2. I clarify roles and responsibilities.

_____ 3. I define priorities.

_____ 4. I take a stand for my values.

_____ 5. I deal with issues and concerns promptly.

_____ 6. I challenge others to make right choices.

_____ 7. I make tough decisions regardless of people's approval or rejection.

_____ 8. I prefer to work on tasks with a team rather than individually.

_____ 9. I regularly build team spirit and morale and get results.

_____ 10. I encourage interaction and collaboration among team members.

_____ 11. I lead the celebration of team accomplishments.

_____ 12. To get diverse perspectives, I solicit input from my team members.

_____ 13. I actively involve others in the change process.

_____ 14. I motivate others to embrace change.

_____ 15. I identify and seek to tap people's potential.

_____ 16. I consider and offer developmental challenges.

_____ 17. I find ways to support and encourage others.

_____ 18. I inspire and provoke others to excel.

_____ 19. I trust in people's competence.

_____ 20. I establish high performance standards.

_____ 21. I lead by setting a positive example that inspires others.

_____ 22. I reward performance and provide constructive feedback.

(Continued)

_____ 23. I initiate relationships with others.

_____ 24. I work effectively with others who are different from me.

_____ 25. I prioritize successful resolution of conflict with others.

_____ 26. I keep others informed about what I am doing if it affects them.

_____ 27. I value the heart, character, and integrity of myself and others.

_____ 28. I follow through on the promises and commitments that I make.

_____ 29. I am open to making significant changes in my behavior when necessary.

_____ 30. I am able to exert self-discipline when needed.

Specific examples of ways in which I have demonstrated my leadership skills and abilities over the past 12 months include:

_____
_____
_____
_____
_____
_____
_____
_____
_____

Leadership skills or attributes I would like to develop include: _____

_____
_____
_____
_____

To further develop my leadership skills, I will: _____

_____
_____
_____
_____
_____
_____
_____
_____

Identifying Leaders

Activity F
Chapter 3

Name _____

Date _____ Period _____

For this activity, you will be identifying the leadership styles of four characters in a movie of your choice. After choosing your movie, identify four characters that you think demonstrate leadership. Write these characters' names in the following table. Next, using the information on leadership from the textbook and your notes, determine each character's leadership style, citing specific examples of proof from the movie to support your leadership style claim. Remember, leaders often use more than one leadership style, depending on the situation. After filling out the table, answer the questions at the end of the activity.

Movie choice: _____

Character 1	
Character name	
Leadership style(s)	
Specific examples of leadership style(s)	

Character 2	
Character name	
Leadership style(s)	
Specific examples of leadership style(s)	

Character 3	
Character name	
Leadership style(s)	

(Continued)

Specific examples of leadership style(s)	
Character 4	
Character name	
Leadership style(s)	
Specific examples of leadership style(s)	

1. Who do you think was the most effective leader in the movie? Why? Provide examples that show the leader you have chosen to be the best.

   _____
   _____
   _____
   _____
   _____
   _____
   _____

2. Compare and contrast the leadership styles of two other characters in the movie. Which one is more effective? Why?

   _____
   _____
   _____
   _____
   _____
   _____
   _____
   _____

Chapter 4: On the Road to Personal and Professional Success

Good Grooming

Activity A
Chapter 4

Name _____
Date _____ Period _____

Personal grooming involves taking care of your body and general appearance. Think about your grooming habits as you respond to the following questions. After answering the questions, identify any grooming habits you might like to change.

1. How do you care for your skin? _____
   _____

2. How often do you bathe or shower? _____

3. How often do you shave? _____

4. During what times of the day do you avoid exposure to the sun? _____
   _____

5. How do you protect your skin when you are in the sun? _____
   _____

6. How often do you need to shampoo your hair? _____

7. What type of shampoo do you use? _____

8. How often do you get your hair cut? _____

9. How often do you check your weight? _____

10. How often do you go to the dentist? _____

11. How often do you get your vision checked? _____

12. What daily care do you give to your hands and feet? _____

13. What weekly care do you give to your hands and feet? _____

14. What daily care do you give to your hair? _____
    _____

15. What weekly care do you give to your hair? _____
    _____

16. How often do you eat junk food? _____

17. How often do you eat healthy snacks? _____

Healthy or Hazardous?

Activity B
Chapter 4

Name_____

Date_____ Period _____

Avoiding health hazards is a very important way to promote wellness. When energy is boosted, increased productivity often follows. For this activity, work with a partner or in small groups to answer the questions about health hazards in Part 1. Then complete the activity in Part 2.

Part 1

1. Which health hazard discussed in the text—tobacco, alcohol, or other drugs—do you think poses the greatest risk to teens? Why?
   _____
   _____
   _____

2. Why do you believe teens are willing to take risks with their health? _____
   _____
   _____

3. What would you tell a friend who was engaged in risky behavior that could affect his or her health?
   _____
   _____
   _____

Part 2

Create a commercial to convey the message you identified in #3. Use the space below to record your list of characters and summarize the storyline. Film your commercial and show it to the class. Write a summary indicating how your audience reacted to the commercial.

Characters:_____
_____
_____

Storyline: _____
_____
_____
_____

Audience reaction: _____
_____
_____

Ethics in the Workplace

Activity C
Chapter 4

Name_____

Date_____ Period _____

In the workplace, employees are constantly making ethical decisions that affect their employers, coworkers, and clients. Sometimes making ethical decisions is easy. Oftentimes, however, making ethical decisions is difficult and complex. Not all situations present clear-cut ethical issues. Instead, some situations may fall within "gray areas."

Working in small groups, read and discuss the following scenarios. Identify the ethical issue/problem for each scenario and what you would choose to do in the same situation. Be prepared to discuss your reasoning for making that choice in class.

Scenario 1 *Ellie is an administrative assistant in the human resources department of a large company. Her good friend Madison is applying for a job with the company, and Ellie has agreed to serve as a reference for her. Madison calls Ellie for advice on preparing for the interview. Ellie has the actual questions that will be asked of everyone interviewing for the job. Should Ellie make a copy of the questions so Madison can adequately prepare?*

Identify the ethical issue/problem: _____

_____

_____

What do you do and why? _____

_____

_____

_____

_____

Scenario 2 *Akemi is an office worker in the facilities management department. He has just received a new computer and wants to try it out. Though his supervisor has a strict policy about computer use for business purposes only, Akemi wants to learn the e-mail software more thoroughly than his training can provide. He figures the best way to learn the new software is to write e-mail messages to his friends and relatives until he feels comfortable with the program. Akemi is caught up on all his work and only has 30 minutes left in his workday. His supervisor left early.*

Identify the ethical issue/problem: _____

_____

_____

What do you do and why? _____

_____

_____

_____

_____

(Continued)

Scenario 3 *Jaden was recently hired to work as a receptionist in the front lobby. As the receptionist, she is responsible for making copies for the associates. Her son, Luis, comes in and needs some copies for a school project. He brought his own paper and needs 300 copies for his class. If he does not bring the copies with him, he will fail the project. The company copier does not require a security key nor do they keep track of copies made by departments.*

Identify the ethical issue/problem: _____

_____

_____

What do you do and why? _____

_____

_____

_____

_____

_____

Scenario 4 *Michael applied for the position of sales manager. You had human resources check his references. It is difficult to read his application because his handwriting is so messy. You are considering not hiring him because of this. Is this being fair?*

Identify the ethical issue/problem: _____

_____

_____

What do you do and why? _____

_____

_____

_____

_____

_____

Professional Organization Research

Activity D   Name _____

Chapter 4   Date _____ Period _____

Working in small groups, research a professional organization that you could join in your career interest area. Fill in the following information about the organization you researched.

1. Name of organization: _____

2. Search engine used: _____

3. Website address: _____

4. List 10 facts of important information that you found from this site; this might include membership cost, how long they have been around, any publications they have, opportunities for members, etc.

   Fact 1: _____
   _____

   Fact 2: _____
   _____

   Fact 3: _____
   _____

   Fact 4: _____
   _____

   Fact 5: _____
   _____

   Fact 6: _____
   _____

   Fact 7: _____
   _____

   Fact 8: _____
   _____

   Fact 9: _____
   _____

   Fact 10: _____
   _____

5. How can you use this information to help you in your future career? _____
   _____
   _____

Can You Manage Your Time Wisely?

Activity E
Chapter 4

Name_____

Date_____ Period _____

People with good time management skills are efficient and productive. They plan their time wisely so they can get everything done that they want to do. This activity, which will take a week to complete, will test your time management skills. At the beginning of the week, complete the activity in Part 1. At the end of the week, answer the questions in Part 2.

Part 1

For one week, use a planner or organizer to schedule your time. Start by entering your regularly scheduled activities, such as school and afterschool activities. Then, determine what other activities you have to do this week. Prioritize these additional items and identify how much time you will need to complete each task. Enter the additional activities into your planner. As you go through your week, cross out items you complete in the time allotted.

Part 2

1. Were you able to complete all your activities in the time allotted? If not, which days were you unable to meet your goals?
   _____

2. Did any unexpected events throw your schedule off? How did you manage to adjust your schedule? Explain.
   _____
   _____
   _____
   _____
   _____
   _____

3. How did your personal priorities influence which time commitments were met?_____
   _____
   _____
   _____
   _____

4. Did you find that keeping track of your activities helped you manage your time better? Why or why not?
   _____
   _____
   _____
   _____

Rate Your Stress

Activity F
Chapter 4

Name _____

Date _____ Period _____

Some stress is necessary for life, but too much stress can be harmful. A scale has been developed for measuring stress in terms of life's daily events. The following table is adapted to a teenager's life. To find your score, add the correct point value to the "My Score" column for all events applying to you during the past 12 months. Then tally your points. A score of 300+ means you have an 80 percent chance of negatively impacting wellness. After totaling your points, answer the questions at the end of the activity.

Event	Point Value	My Score
Death of a parent or other significant adult	100	
Divorce of parents	73	
Marital separation of parents	65	
Jail term for you	63	
Death of close family member	63	
Personal injury or illness	53	
Marriage	50	
Fired from your full-time work	47	
Marital reconciliation of parents	45	
Remarriage of parents	45	
Change in family member's health	44	
Pregnancy	40	
Received low grades	39	
Addition to your family	39	
Breaking up of a relationship	39	
A change in your financial status	38	
Death of a close friend	37	
Getting a part-time job	36	
Change in the number of family arguments	35	
Fired from a part-time job	31	
Changing jobs	30	
A change in work or school responsibilities	29	
Brother or sister leaving home	29	
Trouble with parents or siblings	29	

(Continued)

Outstanding personal achievement	29	
Trouble with school	26	
Starting or finishing school	26	
A change in living conditions	26	
A change in personal habits	24	
Trouble with your boss	23	
Change in working hours, conditions	20	
Change in residence	20	
Change in school	20	
Change in recreation habits	19	
Change in religious activities	19	
Change in social activities	18	
Disagreement with a friend	17	
Change in sleeping habits	16	
Change in number of family gatherings	15	
Change in eating habits	15	
Vacation	13	
The Christmas season	12	
Minor violation of the law	11	
MY TOTAL POINTS:		

1. What does this information say about the amount of stress in your life? _____
   _____
   _____
   _____
   _____
   _____

2. What activities do you engage in to help relieve stress? _____
   _____
   _____
   _____
   _____
   _____

Chapter 5
Looking Inward: Identifying Your Personal Brand

Graffiti Wall Activity

Activity A
Chapter 5

Name _____

Date _____ Period _____

Everyone has an idea of who they are, but how do they project who they are so that others can see? Companies do this by having a brand that everyone recognizes. People can do this as well. Using the brick wall below, create a graffiti wall that explains who you are. This is the first step in understanding your current personal brand.

If you have trouble, ask yourself the following questions:

- Am I short or tall?
- Who is my best friend?
- How would I describe my eyes?
- How am I like my best friend?
- What is my greatest strength?

- What activities do I enjoy?
- What is my greatest weakness?
- What is my favorite color?
- What is my favorite hobby?
- How am I like my parents?

Olena Kravchenko/Shutterstock.com

Interpersonal Skills Inventory

Activity B
Chapter 5

Name _____

Date _____ Period _____

Completing assessments and inventories can be a good way to help you get to know yourself and identify your own personal brand. For this activity, read and think about each statement carefully, and respond as honestly as possible. Then, assess your responses.

Most of the Time	Sometimes	Rarely	
_____	_____	_____	1. I tend to do most of the talking in conversations.
_____	_____	_____	2. I am able to resolve problems without losing control of my emotions.
_____	_____	_____	3. When talking to people, I pay attention to their body language.
_____	_____	_____	4. I get so caught up in what I have to say that I am unaware of the reactions of my listeners.
_____	_____	_____	5. When I know what someone is going to say, I finish the sentence for him or her.
_____	_____	_____	6. I tend to fall asleep when someone is presenting.
_____	_____	_____	7. I fidget (e.g., play with hair, watch, pen) when listening to someone talking.
_____	_____	_____	8. I tend to not speak when I am dealing with someone I find intimidating.
_____	_____	_____	9. I change the way I talk depending on who I am speaking with (e.g., I speak more professionally when I am in a meeting).
_____	_____	_____	10. If I have something relevant to add, I will interrupt someone to make certain my views are heard.
_____	_____	_____	11. People complain that I do not appear to be listening when they speak to me.
_____	_____	_____	12. I try to divert or end conversations that do not interest me.

Which response in your inventory is the most frustrating for you? Why?_____
_____

Which response in your inventory do you think affects those around you the most? Why?_____
_____
_____

If you could change or improve one of your responses in the inventory, which one would it be? How would you change it?
_____
_____

Celebrating Personal Accomplishments

Activity C
Chapter 5

Name _____

Date _____ Period _____

At this stage of your life, you should begin thinking about a career choice. The following questions will help you focus on what you have already accomplished in your life. In the spaces provided, list any awards and achievements you have received in school, in the community, through volunteer work, or in other extracurricular activities. You can then use this information to identify types of careers you might like to pursue.

1. What awards and recognition have you received in school? _____
   _____
   _____
   _____
   _____
   _____
   _____

2. What awards and recognition have you received in your local community? _____
   _____
   _____
   _____
   _____
   _____
   _____

3. What volunteer work have you performed? List any awards or recognition you have received through volunteer work.
   _____
   _____
   _____
   _____
   _____
   _____

4. What clubs and organizations are you involved in through school as well as outside of school? List any awards or recognition you have received through these organizations.
   _____
   _____
   _____
   _____
   _____
   _____

Who Is Your Mentor?

Activity D
Chapter 5

Name _____

Date _____ Period _____

Whenever you look up to someone to emulate or because you believe in what they are doing, you are viewing that person as a mentor. There are two types of mentors: an official mentor and an unofficial mentor. An *official mentor* is a person who guides you, models appropriate behaviors and attitudes, and takes an active role in your development. An *unofficial mentor* serves as a model who is worthy of imitation, even though the person may not know it. Using these definitions for the two types of mentors, answer the following questions.

1. Who in your life is an official mentor? _____

2. Why is this person your official mentor? Give an example of how this person has mentored you in your daily life.
   _____
   _____
   _____

3. Who in your life is an unofficial mentor? _____

4. Why is this person your unofficial mentor? Give an example of how this person has influenced you in your daily life.
   _____
   _____
   _____

5. Do you have anyone who you mentor? If so, what do you do to help him or her become a better person?
   _____
   _____
   _____

6. If you were able to meet any famous person, who would it be, and why? _____
   _____
   _____
   _____

7. What would you tell this famous person about his or her actions and how he or she influences yourself and the next generation?
   _____
   _____

What Would You Do?

Activity E
Chapter 5

Name _____

Date _____ Period _____

Each day in your life you make decisions. Some decisions you make consciously while others you make without even realizing it. Read through the following scenarios and then decide what you think the person should do. Be sure to explain why this is the best decision in the given situation.

Scenario 1 *Zoe is not happy with her weight. All of her friends are on various diets, but her parents do not believe teenagers should diet because their bodies are still growing and they think that dieting could harm their growth. Zoe's parents have suggested she could eat smaller portions and exercise more to work on her weight. A friend has told Zoe she has a pill that will help her lose weight quickly, and because she bought too many, she would sell her some at a reduced cost.*

What should Zoe do? Why? _____

_____

_____

_____

_____

Scenario 2 *Myka loves to go clothes shopping. She looks forward to her trips when she is able to try on new outfits and styles. For her birthday, her grandmother gave her $100 to spend on clothes. Myka has been looking around and she can get two outfits for the $100 or she can buy one pair of designer jeans.*

What should Myka do? Why? _____

_____

_____

_____

_____

Scenario 3 *Aristeo was a premature baby who got sick a lot growing up. Out of fear for their son's health, Aristeo's parents refuse to let him participate in sports. Without telling his parents, Aristeo signed up to try out for the school soccer team, and made it. There are forms that have to be signed by his parents and returned to the coach. Aristeo has thought about forging his parent's signature or having one of his friends do it for him, but he is afraid of being caught when he has to tell his parents why he is staying after school for practice and games.*

What should Aristeo do? Why? _____

_____

_____

_____

_____

(Continued)

Scenario 4 Nikko has always had to share a room with his younger brother growing up. His parents are talking about buying a new house and have asked him if he minds sharing with his younger brother or if he wants to have his own room. Nikko had told his parents that it really did not matter to him either way, but as he has thought about it over the last few days, he likes the idea of having his own room. Nikko's parents are about to make a bid for a house where he would have to share a room with his brother.

What should Nikko do? Why? _____

_____

_____

_____

_____

Scenario 5 Jacob, who is in his senior year of high school, has been dating Aubrey, a junior, for six months. Yesterday, Aubrey came to Jacob and told him she was pregnant. Today, he found out that Aubrey had also been seeing two other guys during the time they were dating. Aubrey is insisting that the baby is his and not the other boys. Jacob has talked things over with his parents and they believe that a paternity test should be done after the baby is born to determine parentage. Aubrey has refused, saying Jacob should trust what she is telling him and that if he insists she will make sure he does not have any contact with the baby.

What should Jacob do? Why? _____

_____

_____

_____

_____

Scenario 6 Kelly was walking through the hallway at school and noticed several people picking on another student. Some of the things they were saying to this girl were not only mean, but disgusting and degrading as well. Kelly knows that if she says anything she will become a target for the school bullies, too. However, her parents have instilled in her a characteristic trait of standing up for those who are unable to do so themselves. Kelly can either confront the bullies herself or get an adult to intervene. She worries that if she goes to get an adult, the bullies might not be caught in the act of what they are doing. Kelly thinks about using her cell phone to record what is going on and then turning the information in to her principal.

What should Kelly do? Why? _____

_____

_____

_____

_____

Setting My Goals

Activity F
Chapter 5

Name _____

Date _____ Period _____

Identify three long-term goals you have in your life. For each long-term goal, identify the short-term and immediate goals you will need to accomplish to help you reach your long-term goals. Remember, your goals should be S.M.A.R.T. goals.

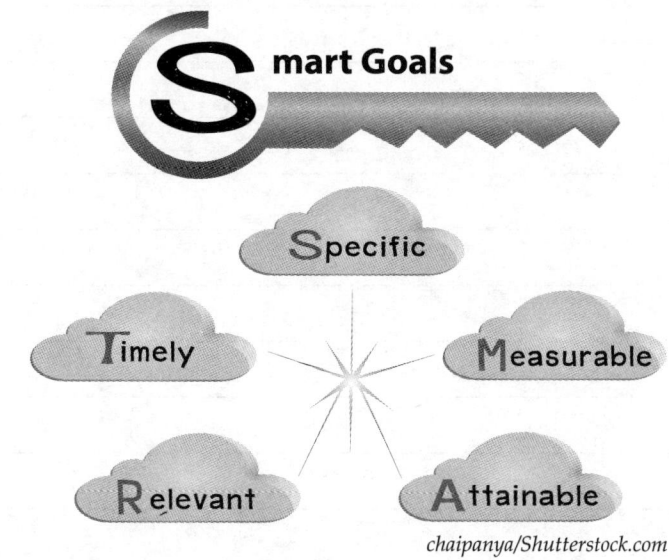

chaipanya/Shutterstock.com

Goal #1

Long-term goal: _____

_____

Deadline: _____

Short-term goal: _____

_____

Immediate goal: _____

_____

Immediate goal: _____

_____

Short-term goal: _____

_____

Immediate goal: _____

_____

Immediate goal: _____

_____

(Continued)

Goal #2

Long-term goal: _____
_____

Deadline: _____

Short-term goal: _____
_____

Immediate goal: _____
_____

Immediate goal: _____
_____

Short-term goal: _____
_____

Immediate goal: _____
_____

Immediate goal: _____
_____

Goal #3

Long-term goal: _____
_____

Deadline: _____

Short-term goal: _____
_____

Immediate goal: _____
_____

Immediate goal: _____
_____

Short-term goal: _____
_____

Immediate goal: _____
_____

Immediate goal: _____
_____

Chapter 6: Looking Outward: Connecting with Human Services

Gaining Firsthand Knowledge

Activity A
Chapter 6

Name _____

Date _____ Period _____

Gaining hands-on experience in a career field of interest enables you to get a close-up look into what a job involves. In this activity, match the following terms to their appropriate definitions. Then, identify places in your community where you would be interested in gaining firsthand knowledge.

Definitions

_____ 1. Paid or unpaid work with emphasis placed on learning over performance.

_____ 2. Giving of your time without compensation.

_____ 3. Able to make key contacts with professionals in your field of interest.

_____ 4. Opportunity to talk with some of the key professionals in your field of interest.

_____ 5. Short observation consisting of a few hours or a day.

_____ 6. Short-term investment of time and energy.

_____ 7. Differ from regular jobs in that they often offer a more in-depth look at management decision making and practices.

_____ 8. Valuable experience to put onto a résumé.

_____ 9. Have a list of questions prepared beforehand.

_____ 10. Company agrees to provide an opportunity to gain exposure to an occupational area.

Terms

A. informational interview
B. internship
C. job shadowing
D. volunteering

Community Examples

_____
_____
_____
_____
_____
_____

Understanding the *Occupational Outlook Handbook*

Activity B
Chapter 6

Name _____

Date _____ Period _____

The *Occupational Outlook Handbook* (OOH) is a publication created by the Bureau of Labor Statistics to help people learn about careers. It can be found at www.bls.gov/ooh. Using the website and your textbook, identify what information is available for use in the *Occupational Outlook Handbook* by responding to the following questions and statements.

1. What specific information is available on the OOH website? _____
_____
_____

2. How often is the OOH updated? _____

3. Why would it be important to know the typical job duties of a career? _____
_____
_____

4. What information will help you identify how well your needs, interests, and goals match the requirements of a career or industry?
_____
_____

5. What type of salary information is provided on the website? _____
_____

6. Why would it be important to consider the geographic location and relative cost of living when you are looking at salary and wage information?
_____
_____
_____

7. The more information you have about a job market, the better equipped you will be to make a decision about a career choice. What information is available under the projected job outlook heading to help you in your decision making?
_____
_____
_____

8. What factors would need to be present in a company's work environment for you to want to work there?
_____
_____
_____

Researching with the *Occupational Outlook Handbook*

Activity C
Chapter 6

Name _____

Date _____ Period _____

The *Occupational Outlook Handbook* is a good source of career guidance information. Knowing how to navigate and find information on this website can be helpful in searching for a job or information about a career. To begin, choose an occupation that you would like to learn more about. Then, using the OOH website, find the following information about this career in the *Occupational Outlook Handbook*.

1. Name of career I am researching: _____

2. Why am I interested in this career? _____
   _____
   _____
   _____

3. What education beyond high school is required for this career? _____
   _____
   _____

4. What important qualities should workers in this occupation possess? _____
   _____
   _____
   _____
   _____

5. What are the major duties and activities of workers in this occupation? _____
   _____
   _____
   _____
   _____
   _____
   _____
   _____

6. What specific skills do I need to perform this career? _____
   _____
   _____
   _____
   _____
   _____

7. What is the beginning salary for this career? _____

8. What are the working hours and conditions of this career? _____
_____
_____

9. What are the opportunities for advancement in this career field? _____
_____
_____
_____

10. Where is the greatest opportunity to be employed in this career located? _____
_____
_____

11. Is the work environment of this career dangerous? If so, how? _____
_____

12. Does this career involve travel? If so, how much? _____
_____

13. What is the job outlook for this career? _____
_____
_____
_____
_____

14. Can I live in my hometown to perform this job? If so, where could I work? _____
_____
_____

15. What are some similar occupations? _____
_____
_____
_____
_____

16. After researching this career, are you still interested in it? Why or why not? _____
_____
_____
_____

Choosing Classes in School

Activity D
Chapter 6

Name _____

Date _____ Period _____

Maximizing your high school experience will help you reach your future goals. Many classes help you prepare for a future career; this class is one example. Review the following terms and their definitions, and then answer the questions based on your school's process for choosing classes each year.

Terms
Program of study—guide that shows the core and career-related courses a person needs to take to follow his or her career path.
Advanced placement courses—high school classes that offer college level content and exams; students receive college credit for successful completion.
Dual credit courses—college or university classes that students take while still attending high school; students receive college credit for successful completion.

1. Identify the career pathway in which you are currently enrolled. _____
_____

2. List the core and career-related courses you need to take your freshman year of high school.
_____
_____
_____
_____
_____

3. List the core and career-related courses you need to take your sophomore year of high school.
_____
_____
_____
_____
_____

4. List the core and career-related courses you need to take your junior year of high school.
_____
_____
_____
_____
_____

5. List the core and career-related courses you need to take your senior year of high school.
   _____
   _____
   _____
   _____
   _____

6. What advanced placement courses, if any, does your school offer that you could take? When could you take them?
   _____
   _____
   _____
   _____
   _____

7. What prerequisites, if any, must you meet before taking an advanced placement course at your school?
   _____
   _____
   _____
   _____
   _____

8. What dual credit courses does your school offer that you could take? When could you take them?
   _____
   _____
   _____
   _____

9. What prerequisites, if any, must you complete before taking a dual credit class? _____
   _____
   _____
   _____

10. What additional expenses, if any, would you have to pay when taking a dual credit class?
    _____
    _____
    _____
    _____

Comparing College Costs

Activity E
Chapter 6

Name _____

Date _____ Period _____

College costs can vary based on where you go to school, whether it is a public or private school, and if you are considered in-state or out-of-state for tuition. For this activity, choose two colleges or universities that you are interested in and complete the following table. Then answer the question that follows.

Factors to Compare	School #1	School #2
Location		
Size		
Reputation		
Admission requirements		
Average cost for 15 hours on semester		
What your major would be		

Based on the information provided in the table, which school would you choose to attend? Why?

_____
_____
_____
_____

Student Organization Internet Quest

Activity F

Chapter 6

Name _____

Date _____ Period _____

There are two student organizations that are closely related to the field of human services. Using the Internet, the textbook, and other available resources, complete the following questions.

1. What is the national website for Family, Career and Community Leaders of America (FCCLA)?
   _____

2. What is the cost for membership in FCCLA? _____

3. What competitions would you be interested in participating in with FCCLA? _____
   _____
   _____

4. What FCCLA meetings does your state have? (EX: local, regional) _____
   _____
   _____

5. Does your school have a FCCLA chapter? _____

6. How can you get involved in your local chapter? _____
   _____
   _____

7. What is the website for the Educators Rising group in your state? _____
   _____

8. What is the cost for membership in the Educators Rising group? _____

9. What competitions would you be interested in participating with Educators Rising? _____
   _____
   _____

10. What Educators Rising meetings does your state have? (EX: local, regional) _____
    _____
    _____

11. Does your school have an Educators Rising chapter? _____

12. How can you get involved in your local chapter? _____
    _____
    _____

Chapter 7
Looking Ahead: Preparing for Workplace Success

Investigating Job Openings

Activity A
Chapter 7

Name _____

Date _____ Period _____

Looking for a job can be a daunting experience. Where do you find information, who do you talk to? These are questions every teen asks themselves when they begin the process of looking for a job.

1. Where can you look to find job openings? _____
_____
_____

2. Explain what networking is and how it works. _____
_____
_____
_____

3. What is the key to networking? _____
_____
_____

4. How do you use an Internet job board? _____
_____
_____
_____

5. How can you successfully navigate a job fair? _____
_____
_____
_____

6. Why should you write a thank-you message after talking with people at a job fair? _____
_____
_____
_____

Completing an Application

Activity B　　　　　　　　　　　Name _____

Chapter 7　　　　　　　　　　　Date _____　Period _____

No matter what job you would like to have, you must complete a job application to even be considered for an opening. Use the following application to practice filling one out.

Job Application

Personal Information

Last Name		First Name	Middle Initial
Address		City	State	Zip
How long at present address?	Phone Number		Social Security Number

What date will you be available for work?

Type of employment desired:　　_____ Full-time only　　_____ Part-time only　　_____ Full- or part-time
If hired, can you furnish proof that you are legally entitled to work in the United States?
If hired, can you furnish proof of age?

What position are you applying for?	What are your salary requirements?

Hours you will be available to work:
Have you ever been convicted of a felony?
If yes, please explain
The XYZ Company is a drug-free employer and you will be required to pass a druge sreening as a condition of employment. I understand and agree to participate in testing. (_____) initials

Educational Information

Name and Address of School	Course of Study	Diploma or Degree
High School		
College Education		
Graduate Education		
Other Education/Training		

Writing a Résumé

Activity C
Chapter 7

Name _____

Date _____ Period _____

Many employers request that job applicants submit their résumé when filling out an application. Use the following template to record the information you will need to write your résumé.

Contact Information
(Include full name, address, phone number, and e-mail address.)

Objective
(Include a career goal for the type of job for which you would like to be considered.)

Education
(List schools in reverse chronological order, including name and location, dates, diploma or degree earned, and grade point average.)
Example: Hendrickson High School, Pflugerville, Texas; 20XX—present; 3.5 GPA

Work Experience
(Include all paid and volunteer work, use reverse chronological order, include dates, names and locations of companies, and job titles.)
Example: March 20XX–July 20XX; Sonic Drive-In, 1101 FM 685, Pflugerville, Texas 78660; Car Hop

---

(Continued)

Awards, Honors, and Achievements

(List any school or community awards or honors and personal achievements of which you are most proud.)

Work Skills

(List any programs or equipment you can use, as well as personal work ethics.)

Extracurricular Activities, Interests, and Hobbies

(Highlight aspects of your experiences which mean the most to your prospective employer.)

References

(List people who are *not* family that know your strengths. Include name, position or business title, phone number, and e-mail address.)

What Is in a Cover Message?

Activity D
Chapter 7

Name _____

Date _____ Period _____

Writing a cover message is an important part of the résumé process. This message introduces you and explains why you are sending your résumé. Using the local newspaper or an Internet job site, choose one job and write the cover message for the job. Use the following template, as well as information from the textbook, to help you write your cover message. Remember, it is usually three to four paragraphs.

To Whom It May Concern:

_____
_____
_____
_____
_____
_____
_____
_____
_____
_____
_____
_____
_____
_____
_____
_____
_____
_____
_____
_____
_____
_____
_____
_____

Personal Portfolios

Activity E
Chapter 7

Name _____

Date _____ Period _____

Throughout this course, you will be working on various aspects of a personal portfolio to illustrate your accomplishments and strengths. Answer the following questions about portfolios.

1. What do personal portfolios show? _____
   _____
   _____

2. What do effective portfolios have in common? _____
   _____
   _____

3. What are some common items you can include in a portfolio? _____
   _____
   _____
   _____

4. How should you identify items in your portfolio? _____
   _____
   _____

5. What is one of the most common methods of organizing a portfolio? _____
   _____
   _____

6. Why would someone choose to put their portfolio in an electronic format? _____
   _____
   _____
   _____

7. What are some tips to remember about putting together your portfolio? _____
   _____
   _____
   _____

8. Why would it be important to have an error-free portfolio? _____
   _____
   _____

Starting a New Job

Activity F
Chapter 7

Name _____

Date _____ Period _____

The first time someone meets you is when he or she forms a first impression of you. First impressions are the basis on how your new coworkers judge you until you prove them right or wrong. Read and respond to each of the following scenarios. Record your responses in the spaces provided.

Scenario 1 *Joel is interning at World Press Incorporated as an assistant to the Vice President of Marketing. Joel shows up to his first day of work dressed in pressed blue jeans, a button-up shirt with a sports coat, and tennis shoes. Joel arrives 15 minutes early to work and waits in the lobby until it is time to report to his orientation session.*

Did Joel do anything wrong? If so, what does he need to correct? _____

_____

_____

_____

_____

_____

_____

_____

_____

Scenario 2 *Karen is in a rush and does not realize she is wearing one black shoe and one navy blue shoe. She arrives 20 minutes late and misses the meet-and-greet offered to new employees. She does not know where she is supposed to fill out her employment forms and is afraid to ask.*

What should Karen do? What has she done wrong? How can she fix it? _____

_____

_____

_____

_____

_____

_____

_____

_____

Scenario 3 *Carlos has a thyroid problem that causes him to gain weight. His new boss is aware of the problem and told Carlos not to worry about his medical issue. The company will work with him when he needs to go to the doctor. Carlos overheard three of his new coworkers joking about his weight, which causes him to be hurt and embarrassed.*

How should Carlos handle this situation? _____

_____

_____

_____

_____

_____

_____

Scenario 4 *Jessica is in human resources filling out her paperwork when she realizes she forgot to bring her Social Security card and does not know the number. The human resources director is also asking who Jessica wants to list as her emergency contact number. Jessica did not realize she would need anyone's name or number as an emergency contact and does not know who to list.*

What should Jessica do? _____

_____

_____

_____

_____

_____

_____

Scenario 5 *Kyle was given a copy of the employee handbook on his first day of work. In his orientation meeting, they told all new employees that they needed to read and familiarize themselves with the handbook. One of the sections talked about confidentiality of client information. Kyle's job this week was making copies of client information and filing it. When he got home Friday evening, he began to feel like he forgot to take some papers off the copy machine. Kyle can either return to work or call his supervisor and report that he thinks he left papers on the copy machine or he cannot worry about it until Monday.*

What should Kyle do? Explain your answer and why you chose it. _____

_____

_____

_____

_____

_____

Chapter 8 Consumer Services

Careers in Consumer Services

Activity A
Chapter 8

Name _____
Date _____ Period _____

There are various and constantly expanding career opportunities in consumer services. Many of these careers fall into four major tracks. These are consumer advocacy, financial services, customer service, and buying. For this activity, give examples of careers in each area and identify local job opportunities. Then answer the questions that follow.

Consumer Services Career Area	Examples of Careers	Local Job Opportunities
Consumer advocacy		
Financial services		
Customer service		
Buying		

1. Of the local jobs you listed, which one is the most interesting to you? Why? _____
_____
_____

2. Of the local jobs you listed, which one is the least interesting to you? Why? _____
_____
_____

Consumer Rights and Responsibilities

Activity B
Chapter 8

Name _____

Date _____ Period _____

An important responsibility of many consumer services workers is to teach their clients and customers about their consumer rights. In the following table, identify and provide explanations for the rights and responsibilities of consumers. Then answer the questions.

Consumer Rights	Explanations

Consumer Responsibilities	Explanations

1. Why would consumers need to know about their rights and responsibilities? _____
_____
_____

2. When buying items, you may hear the phrase, "Let the buyer beware." How do consumer rights and responsibilities help when consumers have problems with goods and services they purchase?
_____
_____

Evaluating Advertising Claims

Activity C Name _____

Chapter 8 Date _____ Period _____

Advertisers will use many different advertising techniques to try to get consumers to buy their products or services. Consumers must beware, however, that just because a product is advertised, it is not always good for them. To complete this activity, view an ad on television or in print and evaluate it by answering the following questions.

Advertising Techniques
Association—using images in the hope you will transfer your good feelings about the image to the product.
Call to action—telling you what to do, removes all doubt about next steps.
Claim—informing you about how the product works or helps you.
Games and activities—putting the commercial into the form of a game can be a fun way for you to get to know more about a product and spend more time with it.
Humor—using ads that make you laugh can catch your attention and are more memorable.
Hype—using words like "amazing" and "incredible" make products seem really exciting.
Must-have—suggesting that you must have the product to be happy, popular, or satisfied.
Repetition—repeating a message or idea so you remember it.
Sales and price—showing or announcing a discounted price makes a product look better.
Sense appeal—using sights and sounds to appeal to your senses.
Testimonials and endorsements—featuring someone, like a celebrity, saying how the product worked for him or her.

1. Which media form did you use to view the advertisement? _____

2. What product was being advertised? _____

3. What advertising technique was being used to sell the product? _____
   _____

4. What did the ad say or suggest about the product or service? _____
   _____
   _____

5. What did the ad imply about the people who buy the product or service? _____
   _____
   _____

6. After viewing the ad, do you want to buy this product? Why or why not? _____
   _____
   _____
   _____

Writing a Letter of Complaint

Activity D
Chapter 8

Name _____

Date _____ Period _____

Sometimes, consumers are unable to get a satisfactory solution to their problem. When this occurs, they may need to write a complaint letter. For this activity, identify a product or service that you or a family member has bought in the last year that is not performing as expected. Respond to the following questions about the product or service. Then, on a separate piece of paper, use your responses to write a complaint letter to the company that manufactures your product or service.

1. What is the name of the unsatisfactory product or service? _____
_____

2. What is the serial number of the product, if applicable? _____
_____

3. What is the description of the product or service? _____
_____
_____
_____

4. When was the date of purchase? _____

5. Where did you make the purchase? (Be sure to include address.) _____
_____
_____

6. What is your problem with the product or service? _____
_____
_____
_____
_____

7. Do you still have the receipt for the product or service? _____

8. What action do you expect the company to take to resolve the problem? _____
_____
_____
_____
_____

Practicing Customer Service

Activity E
Chapter 8

Name _____

Date _____ Period _____

Customer service representatives are responsible for handling consumer complaints. These professionals know how to calmly and politely resolve consumer issues and problems. Read the following customer service scenarios. Then explain how you would handle each situation.

Scenario 1 *A customer calls and berates you for the poor service he received when doing business with your company. You explain to the customer that you need to know the exact nature of his complaint so you can take care of the problem. The customer then screams at you that you cannot do anything and he wants to talk to your manager.*

What do you do? _____

_____

_____

_____

_____

_____

_____

Scenario 2 *Carrie is on her way to the break room when a customer asks her about the sale price of a pair of shoes on display. Carrie responds, "That's not my department," and continues on her way to the break room.*

What should Carrie have done differently? _____

_____

_____

_____

_____

_____

_____

Scenario 3 *You are a clerk at a shoe store. A customer returns a pair of shoes and wants a refund. The shoes have been worn and the sole is dirty.*

How do you respond? _____

_____

_____

_____

_____

_____

_____

(Continued)

Scenario 4 *You are working at the customer service counter in a department store. A customer is upset because she feels she was ignored by the employees working in the linens department when she was trying to get some help.*

What do you do? _____

_____

_____

_____

_____

_____

_____

Scenario 5 *You answer the phones for a local cable company. A customer calls and is upset because her reception is poor.*

How do you handle the situation? _____

_____

_____

_____

_____

_____

_____

Scenario 6 *You work at a drive-through car wash. A customer returns because he feels his car did not get clean.*

What do you do? _____

_____

_____

_____

_____

_____

_____

Consumer Services Terms

Activity F

Chapter 8

Name _____

Date _____ Period _____

Test your knowledge of consumer services by filling in the blanks in the following statements using the terms listed below.

Terms		
biodegradable	finance charges	revolving credit
budget	income	saving
comparison shopping	installment credit	self-advocacy
consumers	interest	social sustainability
direct deposit	investing	sustainable
electronic banking	noninstallment credit	sustainable purchasing
electronic funds transfer (EFT)	principal	warranty
expenses		

(1)_____ are people who purchase goods and services. Consumer services workers help people solve financial and consumer problems, provide information about consumer rights, and offer guidance for (2)_____.

Consumers are responsible for making wise choices in products. One way to do this is by (3)_____, which involves looking at different makes and models of a product at various stores. Usually, there are time limits for returning products or getting a repair or replacement. A (4)_____ is a written guarantee from the manufacturer that a product is in good condition.

Many consumers are looking to buy (5)_____ products that do not deplete or destroy natural resources. Buying products that benefit environmental, social, or human health is known as (6)_____. Special labels on products enable consumers to identify products that are "greener." A (7)_____ label on a product means that a product can break down or decompose naturally without harming the environment.

In addition to the sustainability of product materials and packaging, many consumers want to make sure the companies from which they are buying are being socially responsible. (8)_____ involves issues such as human rights; fair labor laws; community development; and health, safety, and wellness.

A (9)_____ is a written financial plan to manage income, expenses, and savings. By viewing a written list of planned (10)_____ (goods

(Continued)

and services requiring payment), people can see how they are spending their money. If (11)_____ is equal to expenses, overspending will not occur, but (12)_____ money will not be possible either.

Budgeting is not only about spending to meet needs and wants, but also about saving and (13)_____ for the future. A common way to save money is to open a savings account that earns (14)_____. With this type of savings account, the (15)_____, or original amount invested, will grow over time.

(16)_____ involves using the Internet to access banking services. Through the use of electronic banking, people can instantly check account balances and look at their statements. They can transfer money from one account to another, which is called (17)_____. Many employers offer their employees the option of (18)_____.

Using credit involves buying or borrowing now and paying later. (19)_____ is a cash loan repaid with interest in equal, regular payments. Credit offered by a financial institution or merchant to a consumer is called (20)_____. Most credit cards are a form of (21)_____. With this type of credit, lenders make money through (22)_____, which are fees charged for buying on credit.

Chapter 9 Counseling and Mental Health Services

An Informational Interview

Activity A
Chapter 9

Name _____

Date _____ Period _____

Review the examples of counseling and mental health services careers in Figure 9.1 of the textbook. Select the career area that interests you the most. Then, set up an informational interview with a professional in this career. Remember, when conducting an informational interview, come prepared and dress appropriately. Don't forget to send a thank-you message when you are done. The following questions will help you get started.

1. What is your job title? _____

2. How would you describe your typical day? _____

_____

_____

_____

_____

_____

_____

3. What variations occur in your set routine? _____

_____

_____

_____

_____

_____

4. What do you like (and dislike) about your job? _____

_____

_____

_____

_____

_____

_____

(Continued)

5. How would you describe the work environment? _____
_____
_____
_____

6. How did you get into this career field?_____
_____
_____

7. What skills are needed for this job? _____
_____
_____
_____

8. What education and training is needed for this job? _____
_____
_____
_____

9. What personal qualities do you feel are necessary to do your job effectively?_____
_____
_____
_____

10. What are some examples of problems you have had to solve on the job? How did you solve them?
_____
_____
_____
_____

11. What are some examples of ethical decisions you have made on the job? _____
_____
_____
_____
_____

12. What are the rewards of this job? _____
_____
_____
_____

(Continued)

Name _____

13. What are the demands of this job? _____
_____
_____

14. If you could change anything about your job, what would it be? _____
_____
_____

15. What other professionals do you frequently interact with in this position? _____
_____
_____

16. What are the opportunities for career advancement? _____
_____
_____

17. Which courses do you feel are absolutely necessary to succeed in this job? _____
_____
_____

18. What activities, internships, or volunteer experiences would you recommend? _____
_____
_____
_____

19. How do you keep up with the current trends in this field? _____
_____
_____

20. What advice do you have for me as a student? _____
_____
_____

Other questions/responses: _____
_____
_____
_____
_____

Individual and Family Life Cycle

Activity B
Chapter 9

Name _____
Date _____ Period _____

The average human lifespan in the twenty-first century is 78 years of age. During this time, people pass through eight stages of the life cycle. At the same time, there are six stages they experience when becoming a family. For this activity, read the statements and match them with the corresponding stage of the individual or family life cycle.

The Individual Life Cycle

_____ 1. Riley is in middle school.

_____ 2. Charles is moving into a retirement community.

_____ 3. Ellie is starting kindergarten.

_____ 4. Juan's dad is moving in with Juan and his family because of his advanced age and poor health. Juan is in which stage?

_____ 5. Katie has just graduated from college.

_____ 6. Nevaeh is just learning to walk.

_____ 7. Xavier is in high school and getting his driver's license.

_____ 8. Elon and Jayla just had a baby. The baby is in which stage?

Stages

A. infancy
B. toddlerhood
C. early childhood
D. middle childhood
E. adolescence
F. early adulthood
G. middle adulthood
H. older adulthood

The Family Life Cycle

_____ 1. Caroline becomes a grandma.

_____ 2. Tyler and Alyssa are pregnant with their first child.

_____ 3. Malik and Kya are returning from their honeymoon.

_____ 4. Lin is the last child to leave home. Her parents are now in what stage?

_____ 5. Vanesa is beginning kindergarten. Her parents are now in what stage?

_____ 6. Michael and Sara's first child leaves home to attend college, but they still have two other children at home.

Stages

A. beginning stage
B. childbearing stage
C. parenting stage
D. launching stage
E. mid-years stage
F. aging stage

Coping with Family-Life Crises

Activity C
Chapter 9

Name _____

Date _____ Period _____

Read the following scenarios and explain what the people should do to get through the crisis.

Scenario 1 Mary, a single, unemployed mother with two children, ages 3 and 5 years, becomes ill and needs to be hospitalized. She has few sources of support from family and friends. What can she do?

_____
_____
_____
_____

Scenario 2 Hailey, a 15-year-old, runs away from home after being caught at a party that had drugs and alcohol being served to minors.

_____
_____
_____
_____

Scenario 3 Justin, a 35-year-old, was fired from his job. On the way home, he stopped at the bar and drank too much. When Justin arrived home, he physically assaulted his wife. When his daughter tried to intervene, he hit her, too.

_____
_____
_____
_____

Scenario 4 Mrs. Brice noticed that Jenny has been coming to school with a lot of bruises lately. Today, Jenny showed up with cuts on her face and arms.

_____
_____
_____
_____

Scenario 5 Lisa comes home from school to find her mother packing their belongings. When she asks what is going on, her mother tells her, "Your father and I are getting a divorce and we are moving in with your grandparents two hours from here."

_____
_____
_____
_____
_____
_____

Scenario 6 Isaiah has been caught breaking into his classmates' lunch boxes and eating their food. When asked why, he says there is no food at home.

_____
_____
_____
_____
_____
_____

Scenario 7 Leah, a 40-year-old woman who has a 16-year-old son and a 13-year-old daughter, comes home from a doctor's visit and shares with the family that she has been diagnosed with breast cancer.

_____
_____
_____
_____
_____
_____

Scenario 8 Mike's father has been given a job promotion and transfer to another state. Mike is starting his senior year in a new town and a new school. He misses his friends.

_____
_____
_____
_____
_____
_____

Preparing for Death

Activity D
Chapter 9

Name _____
Date _____ Period _____

After reading the "Preparing for Death" section on pages 251–252 of the textbook, respond to the following questions and statements.

1. Many adults often plan for their passing in a rational and organized way. They may arrange their own funerals or memorial services in advance. They may write their last will or put together an advance directive. Why do you think they would do these things in advance?

   _____
   _____
   _____

2. Explain the two types of advance directives discussed in the textbook. _____
   _____
   _____
   _____
   _____

3. Would you personally have an advance directive? Why or why not? _____
   _____
   _____
   _____

4. Imagine that you have found out that you only have a short period of time left to live. What types of plans would you make in advance? Why?

   _____
   _____
   _____

5. Identify the five common stages people experience when learning to cope with their own impending death.

   _____
   _____
   _____

6. Are the stages of dying the same for everyone? Why or why not?

   _____
   _____
   _____

Identifying the Stages of Grieving

Activity E
Chapter 9

Name _____

Date _____ Period _____

Losing a loved one can be traumatic and often causes strong emotional reactions. Similar to the stages of dying, there are also five stages of grieving. Read the scenarios and identify which stage of grief the person is experiencing. Explain why you believe the person is in this stage of grief. Then, respond to the question at the end of the activity.

Scenario 1 *Joy gets a phone call from her parents telling her that her grandmother has passed away. When Joy hangs up the phone, she just can't believe her grandmother is gone.*

Stage of grief: _____

Explanation: _____

_____

Scenario 2 *Debbie is frustrated by everyone asking her how she is doing. She finally screams at everyone to leave her alone.*

Stage of grief: _____

Explanation: _____

_____

Scenario 3 *John is listless and unable to get motivated. It has been several days since he has gotten out of the house and he sees no reason to leave any time soon.*

Stage of grief: _____

Explanation: _____

_____

Scenario 4 *Gary has finished going through his mother's belongings and has begun to give away items that he and his family do not wish to keep.*

Stage of grief: _____

Explanation: _____

_____

Have you ever gone through the grief process? If so, how long did it take you to reach the acceptance stage? What did you learn about the process by going through it?

_____

_____

_____

_____

Counseling and Mental Health Terms

Activity F
Chapter 9

Name _____

Date _____ Period _____

Using the counseling and mental health terms listed below, fill in the blanks to the statements that follow.

Terms		
addiction	clinical depression	joint custody
advance directives	domestic abuse	Last Will and Testament
adversity	do not resuscitate (DNR) order	life cycle
alcoholism	family-life crisis	lifespan
at risk	family life cycle	living will
bipolar disorder	grief	mortality
child custody	hospice care	resilient
child support		

The term (1)_____ refers to the duration of life for a living organism.

(2)_____ refers to the developmental stages individuals go through during their lives. As individuals get married, they enter into the beginning stage of the (3)_____. This stage lasts until the couple has a child. If the couple never has children, they remain in the beginning stage until they enter the mid-years stage.

Families exist in an ever-changing environment. The changes families go through often cause stress for family members. A (4)_____ occurs when a stressor creates adversity for the family, disrupting family function. Families with strong, healthy relationships and greater resources to draw upon are more (5)_____ when facing hardships than families with poor interpersonal relationships and fewer resources.

People who live below, at, or even near the poverty line often lack the resources to meet their basic needs for food, clothing, shelter, and healthcare. Children from families living in poverty are among those labeled as (6)_____. Education provides the best chance to break the cycle of poverty.

Another hardship families may experience is when a family member has a compulsive physical and/or psychological dependence on a substance or behavior, which is an (7)_____. A physical dependence on alcohol can lead to (8)_____.

(Continued)

Abusing alcohol and other substances can also present a certain risk factor for people to engage in (9)_____, which involves threatening to or inflicting harm on another person with whom they are in a close relationship, such as a family member.

Sometimes, couples may experience conflicts that cannot be resolved and they get divorced. When children are involved, the couple may need to go to court to determine who retains (10)_____. In some cases, parents seek (11)_____, in which both parents provide care and make decisions for the child. (12)_____ is a legally binding agreement that determines the payments a noncustodial parent is to make to financially contribute toward the child's care.

When going through a crisis, sadness is a normal emotion people experience. (13)_____, on the other hand, is much more severe than common feelings of sadness. Loneliness, stress, or feelings of failure or inadequacy are factors. People who experience this feel a sense of hopelessness about the present and future. Medical intervention is necessary to treat this condition. In the latter teen years or early adulthood, (14)_____, also called *manic depression*, may be detected.

Facing death is one of the most significant life events a person experiences. For many, preparing for death involves creating a (15)_____ to name beneficiaries of financial assets. It also involves determining what medical care should be provided if the person is no longer capable of making medical decisions for him- or herself. These decisions are called (16)_____.

A (17)_____ is a legal document informing family and medical workers of preferences for being kept alive by artificial means, or letting them pass when there is no chance of recovery. A (18)_____ lets medical staff know that if a person's heart stops or the person stops breathing, he or she does not want CPR.

The process of dying is difficult for everyone involved, especially if the dying process is extended over time due to illness. (19)_____, given by trained medical professionals, focuses on making a person comfortable in his or her last days and hours of life. (20)_____ describes the mental anguish or sorrow the person's death causes.

Chapter 10 Early Childhood Development and Services

Child Care Match Up

Activity A
Chapter 10

Name _____

Date _____ Period _____

Child care workers provide care for children when parents are busy. They can work in private homes, their own homes, or in child care centers. For this activity, match each statement to its proper child care worker or program.

Statements

_____ 1. A government-funded program that helps prepare low-income three- and four-year-olds for school.

_____ 2. Provides child care in private homes for one family and travels with family, if requested.

_____ 3. Operated in a private home for a small number of children.

_____ 4. Program for children two through four years of age.

_____ 5. Plan activities that build children's curiosity and interest in play.

_____ 6. Provide child care services as part of a cultural exchange program.

_____ 7. A business that runs a child care program for its employees.

_____ 8. Child care that is provided in a center and serves many children.

_____ 9. Supervise children and reinforce educational lessons under the direct supervision of a licensed teacher.

_____ 10. Oversees a center's mission, goals, and programs.

Child Care Workers or Programs

A. au pair
B. center-based child care
C. family child care center
D. Head Start
E. nanny
F. pre-K teacher
G. preschool program
H. program director
I. teacher assistant
J. work-related child care program

Interviewing a Child Caregiver

Activity B
Chapter 10

Name _____

Date _____ Period _____

Interview a child care development and services worker. Find out the responses to the following questions. Share your interview responses with the class.

Name of the person you are interviewing: _____

Place of employment: _____

Ages of children under this person's care: _____

1. What is your job title? _____

2. How long have you worked here? _____

3. What are your responsibilities in your role as caregiver? _____
   _____
   _____
   _____
   _____
   _____

4. What routines do you follow in your caregiving situation? _____
   _____
   _____
   _____
   _____

5. How flexible do you have to be in your day-to-day activities? _____
   _____
   _____
   _____
   _____

6. What do you enjoy the most about working with children? Why? _____
   _____
   _____
   _____

(Continued)

Name _____

7. What do you enjoy the least about working with children? Why? _____
_____
_____

8. What skill do you think is the most important to have for your job? Why? _____
_____
_____

9. In what ways is caring for children stressful and tiring? _____
_____
_____
_____
_____

10. What are the working hours and conditions of your job? _____
_____
_____

11. How did you get into this career field? _____
_____
_____

12. What education and training is needed for this job? _____
_____
_____
_____

13. What personal qualities do you feel are necessary to do your job effectively? _____
_____
_____
_____

14. What are some examples of problems you have had to solve on the job? How did you solve them?
_____
_____
_____
_____
_____

(Continued)

15. If you could change anything about your job, what would it be? _____
_____
_____

16. What other professionals do you frequently interact with in this position? _____
_____
_____

17. What are the opportunities for career advancement? _____
_____
_____

18. Which courses do you feel are absolutely necessary to succeed in this job? _____
_____
_____

19. What activities, internships, or volunteer experiences would you recommend? _____
_____
_____
_____

20. What advice do you have for me as a student? _____
_____
_____
_____

Other questions/responses: _____
_____
_____
_____
_____
_____
_____

Developmental Milestones

Activity C
Chapter 10

Name _____
Date _____ Period _____

When you work with children, you need to be able to identify the typical markers of development for each stage during early childhood. As you complete this activity, remember that not all children develop at the same rate, but they will have each of the milestones.

Milestones

_____ 1. Has a higher attention span.

_____ 2. Recognizes some sounds and voices.

_____ 3. Tries to pronounce and repeat words in surrounding conversations.

_____ 4. Demonstrates separation anxiety.

_____ 5. Walks without assistance.

_____ 6. Exhibits temper tantrums.

_____ 7. Lasts until the sixth birthday.

_____ 8. Progresses in toilet learning.

_____ 9. Engages in parallel play.

_____ 10. Identifies objects and body parts.

_____ 11. Experiences Erikson's social-emotional stage of trust versus mistrust.

_____ 12. Uses discovery to solve problems.

_____ 13. Rides a bike with training wheels.

_____ 14. Begins to exhibit preference for right or left hand.

_____ 15. Experiences Erikson's social-emotional stage of initiative versus guilt.

_____ 16. Cries when wants a need addressed.

_____ 17. Engages in pretend play.

_____ 18. Recognizes own name.

_____ 19. Shows interest in and responds to mirrors.

_____ 20. Develops self-awareness.

_____ 21. Loves to tell stories.

_____ 22. Lasts until first birthday.

_____ 23. Places objects in mouth to learn about them.

_____ 24. Lasts until third birthday.

_____ 25. Experiences Erikson's social-emotional stage of autonomy versus shame and doubt.

Stages

A. infancy
B. toddler years
C. preschool years

Discipline and Parenting Styles

Activity D
Chapter 10

Name _____

Date _____ Period _____

When teaching a child self control, independence, safety, and socially acceptable actions and behaviors, parents and caregivers use guidance and discipline. The approach parents use when guiding and disciplining their children is their parenting style. Using your own words, explain what each of the following terms means, giving an example of each type of discipline.

1. Guidance: _____
   _____
   _____

2. Discipline: _____
   _____
   _____

3. Power assertion: _____
   _____
   _____

4. Love withdrawal: _____
   _____
   _____

5. Induction: _____
   _____
   _____

6. Authoritarian style: _____
   _____
   _____

7. Permissive style: _____
   _____
   _____

8. Authoritative style: _____
   _____
   _____

Creating a Safe Environment

Activity E
Chapter 10

Name _____

Date _____ Period _____

Parents and caregivers are responsible for meeting many needs of their children. One important need is to keep children safe. Parents and caregivers do this by childproofing the children's environment. Using information from your textbook and reliable online resources, identify two specific examples of how caregivers create a safe environment for children depending on their children's current developmental stage. Share your examples with other members of the class.

Developmental Stages	Specific Examples
Newborns	1. 2.
Infants	1. 2.
Toddlers	1. 2.
Preschoolers	1. 2.

Identifying Child Abuse

Activity F
Chapter 10

Name _____

Date _____ Period _____

Research the following questions and report the answers and information you found. Make sure to use school-appropriate websites.

1. What is *child abuse*? _____

   _____

2. What is *child neglect*? _____

   _____

3. What is the key difference between *child abuse* and *child neglect*? _____

   _____

4. What are potential effects of child abuse? _____

   _____

   _____

5. What factors may lead to child abuse? _____

   _____

   _____

6. What are the consequences of someone who is charged with child abuse in my state? _____

   _____

7. How have child protection laws in my state changed in the last century? _____

   _____

   _____

   _____

8. Why do you feel child abuse continues to be a problem in society today? _____

   _____

9. What do parents need to do to refrain from abusing children? _____

   _____

My sources: _____

_____

_____

_____

Chapter 11 Family and Community Services

Exploring Careers in Family and Community Services

Activity A
Chapter 11

Name _____

Date _____ Period _____

There are many career opportunities for family and community services workers. Using your textbook, explain what each of the following careers involves and how these family and community services workers meet the needs of their clients. Then, choose one of these careers to research further. Explore reliable career resources online to learn as much as you can about the career. Share your findings with the rest of the class.

1. Social and human services assistants: _____
_____
_____

2. Community health workers: _____
_____
_____

3. Emergency and relief workers: _____
_____
_____

4. Caseworkers: _____
_____
_____

5. Social workers: _____
_____
_____

6. Volunteer coordinators: _____
_____
_____

7. Program and executive directors: _____
_____
_____

Family Structures

Activity B
Chapter 11

Name _____

Date _____ Period _____

Today, families form in a number of ways. For this activity, identify which family structure is being described in each of the following statements.

Descriptions

_____ 1. Alvar and Francisca are married and have no children.

_____ 2. Kira divorced Dmitry and the children live with her. Dmitry moved to another state for his job.

_____ 3. After being married for five years, Meilin and Chao have a baby.

_____ 4. Carmen has two children from a previous marriage. She meets Ignacio and they date for a while and, after discovering they have a lot in common, decide to get married.

_____ 5. Tom and Melissa are unable to have children of their own. They want to work with children so they take children into their home who are unable to live with their biological parents for different reasons.

_____ 6. After fostering a child for two years, the biological parent gives up his or her rights. Ashanti and Jamal go to court to become the child's new parents.

_____ 7. Devi lives at home with her parents. Recently, her grandmother has moved in with them because she is unable to take care of herself anymore.

_____ 8. Laney got pregnant as a teenager. Her ex-boyfriend wants nothing to do with her or the baby.

_____ 9. Corey is a widower with two children. Jennifer is divorced with one child. Corey and Jennifer have been dating for two years and decide to get married.

_____ 10. Jerry and Kathy have been living with their aunt and uncle because their mother passed away and their father is in jail.

Family Structures

A. adoptive family
B. childless family
C. extended family
D. foster family
E. nuclear family
F. single-parent family
G. stepfamily

Functions of the Family

Activity C
Chapter 11

Name _____

Date _____ Period _____

Families serve multiple functions. One of the main functions is to socialize family members into their assigned roles. For this activity, list your roles in the spaces provided.

Types of Roles	My Roles
Inherited roles are given to you based on being born (son, daughter, etc.)	
Assigned roles are those given to you based on different criteria (age, birth order, ethnicity, etc.)	
Chosen roles are those that you take on (friend, helper, club member, etc.)	
Shared roles are those that you share with another person (team member, parent, spouse, etc.)	

Finding Community Resources

Activity D
Chapter 11

Name _____

Date _____ Period _____

Family and community services workers must keep current with social services resources within their community. Their job is to know what resources are available and how to obtain these resources for individuals and families in need. For each resource in the table, find a place in your community that provides the necessary resource to meet clients' needs. Then, identify how clients can obtain this resource.

Resource	Available Community Resources	How to Obtain Community Resources
Food		
Shelter		
Clothing		
Financial relief		
Technology		
Government assistance		

Public Policy and Families

Activity E

Chapter 11

Name _____

Date _____ Period _____

Over the years, guidelines, laws, and regulations have helped improve quality of life for families. As a citizen, there are many ways to be actively involved in public policy change, including voting, campaigning, or supporting the issues. Read the following issues and research supporting and opposing views and potential effects on families. Then, give your opinion on each issue. Explain your choice. Be sure to cite your sources.

Issue 1 *Current law prohibits students who have a prior conviction for drug use, drug possession, or drug dealing to receive federally subsidized student loans for college. Should this remain a law? Why or why not?*

Supporting view: _____

_____

_____

Opposing view: _____

_____

_____

My opinion: _____

_____

_____

_____

Issue 2 *Forces of nature, such as hurricanes, tornadoes, floods, and wildfires, create much devastation and can destroy cities. Should the federal, state, and local governments help victims of these disasters rebuild in the same area or encourage them to relocate to a different area?*

Supporting view: _____

_____

_____

Opposing view: _____

_____

_____

My opinion: _____

_____

_____

_____

(Continued)

Issue 3 *In the past, college students could easily apply for credit cards. Now, federal credit card law requires people under 21 years of age to have a cosigner when applying for a credit card or, if applying independently, to show evidence that they can pay for the card. Do you agree with this legislation? Why or why not?*

Supporting view: _____
_____
_____

Opposing view: _____
_____
_____

My opinion: _____
_____
_____

Issue 4 *The Entertainment Software Ratings Board (ESRB) regulates violence in video games and rates games for age appropriateness. The majority of legislative bodies rely on retailers and parents to enforce these regulations. Do you think the game rating system is effective or do parents buy the games for their children regardless of the ratings? Should the government be able to regulate the distribution of violent video games to minors?*

Supporting view: _____
_____
_____

Opposing view: _____
_____
_____

My opinion: _____
_____
_____

Issue 5 *Some potential life-saving drugs, such as cancer drugs, can be extremely expensive, making it difficult for the average person to afford them. Do you think the government should regulate pharmaceutical drug pricing? What about the expense of drug research and development?*

Supporting view: _____
_____
_____

Opposing view: _____
_____
_____

(Continued)

Name _____

My opinion: _____
_____
_____

Issue 6 *Marketers of food products will often use popular characters on packaging or other tactics to appeal to children. Should the marketing of unhealthy foods to children be restricted or banned?*

Supporting view: _____
_____
_____

Opposing view: _____
_____
_____

My opinion: _____
_____
_____

Issue 7 *Standardized tests have been and continue to be used as a way to measure student performance and teacher effectiveness. These tests are also used in the college admission process. Should schools continue to use standardized testing?*

Supporting view: _____
_____
_____

Opposing view: _____
_____
_____

My opinion: _____
_____
_____

My Sources

_____
_____
_____
_____

Volunteer Hours Sheet

Activity F
Chapter 11

Name _____

Date _____ Period _____

One way of getting on-the-job experience is by volunteering. When working in the family and community services area of human services, there are many opportunities for gaining volunteer hours. By putting this information on a résumé or job application, you show perspective employers that you have skills they can use at their business. Use the following template to record your volunteer experience.

Date	Description of Activities	Time In	Time Out	Total Hours	Signature

Chapter 12 Personal Care Services

An Informational Interview

Activity A

Chapter 12

Name _____

Date _____ Period _____

Review the examples of personal care services careers in Figure 12.1 of the textbook. Select the career area that interests you the most. Then, set up an informational interview with a professional in this career. Remember, when conducting an informational interview, come prepared and dress appropriately. Don't forget to send a thank-you message when you are done. The following questions will help you get started.

1. What is your job title? _____

2. How would you describe your typical day? _____
   _____
   _____
   _____
   _____

3. What variations occur in your set routine? _____
   _____
   _____
   _____

4. What do you like (and dislike) about your job? _____
   _____
   _____
   _____
   _____
   _____

5. How would you describe the work environment? _____
   _____
   _____
   _____

(Continued)

6. How did you get into this career field? _____
_____
_____

7. What skills are needed for this job? _____
_____
_____
_____

8. What education, training, licensure, and certification are needed for this job? _____
_____
_____
_____

9. What personal qualities do you feel are necessary to do your job effectively? _____
_____
_____
_____

10. What are some examples of customer service problems you have had to solve on the job? How did you solve them?
_____
_____
_____
_____
_____

11. What types of client records do you have to complete? How do you protect these records?
_____
_____
_____
_____
_____

12. What are the rewards of this job? _____
_____
_____
_____

(Continued)

Name _____

13. What are the demands of this job? _____
_____
_____
_____

14. If you could change anything about your job, what would it be? _____
_____
_____

15. What challenges do you face when communicating with clients? _____
_____
_____

16. What are the opportunities for career advancement? _____
_____
_____

17. Which courses do you feel are absolutely necessary to succeed in this job? _____
_____
_____

18. What activities, internships, or volunteer experiences would you recommend? _____
_____
_____

19. How do you keep up with the current trends in this field? _____
_____
_____

20. What advice do you have for me as a student? _____
_____
_____
_____

Other questions/responses: _____
_____
_____
_____

Helping Hands

Activity B　　　　　　　　　　Name _____

Chapter 12　　　　　　　　　　Date _____ Period _____

As the world population grows older, they may need help with various tasks in their day-to-day life or assistance in a short- or long-term recovery after an illness, injury, surgery, or accident. The people who work with these individuals lend a helping hand in daily activities all the way to total 24-hour care. For this activity, use your textbook and online resources, such as the OOH website, to provide an explanation of what each of the following care workers do.

Care Workers	What They Do
Personal care aides	
Home health aides	
Certified nursing assistants (CNAs)	
Personal assistants	

Writing Obituaries

Activity C   Name _____

Chapter 12   Date _____ Period _____

As a funeral service worker, you interact with families planning the funeral of a loved one. Many times, the funeral director helps the family write an obituary that is placed in the local newspaper, as well as on the funeral home's website. Imagine you are a funeral director, and your job is to help the following families write obituaries for their loved one. Write an obituary for each scenario. Be sure to include what the person has accomplished in his or her life, who he or she will leave behind, and what he or she is known for doing.

Scenario 1 *A 95-year-old gentleman served in both World War I and World War II, receiving a Purple Heart and other medals for his bravery and actions. He leaves behind three children, 12 grandchildren, and 25 great-grandchildren.*

_____
_____
_____
_____
_____
_____
_____
_____
_____

Scenario 2 *A 47-year-old woman worked as a nurse in a hospital and volunteered at a local free health clinic for disadvantaged youth. She lost her battle with breast cancer. She leaves behind her husband, two children, and one sister.*

_____
_____
_____
_____
_____
_____
_____
_____
_____

(Continued)

Scenario 3 *A 16-year-old girl was involved in a car wreck on her way home from school. She spends two months in a coma before finally passing away. She leaves behind her mother and stepfather, two half-brothers, her father and stepmother, and a stepsister.*

_____
_____
_____
_____
_____
_____
_____
_____
_____
_____
_____
_____
_____
_____

Scenario 4 *A 52-year-old English professor and published author died unexpectedly in his sleep. He leaves behind his wife, two children, and one grandchild. His father preceded him in death.*

_____
_____
_____
_____
_____
_____
_____
_____
_____
_____
_____
_____
_____
_____

Name _____

Cosmetology License Requirements

Activity D
Chapter 12

Name _____
Date _____ Period _____

Cosmetologists are licensed professionals who are trained to provide services to enhance a client's personal appearance through the treatment of hair, skin, and nails. Each state has its own licensing requirements to become a cosmetologist. Research what is required to obtain a cosmetology license in your state while answering the following questions.

1. Where can you find information about your state's licensing requirements for cosmetologists? (For any online resources, list specific websites.)

   _____
   _____
   _____

2. Who is in charge of giving licenses in your state? _____
   _____

3. How many hours of instruction are required before taking the operator's written exam? _____

4. Where is the exam offered? _____
   _____

5. What is the cost of the exam? _____

6. What items are needed to take the exam? _____
   _____

7. When can the practice examination be taken? _____
   _____

8. What skills are needed to have a career in cosmetology? _____
   _____
   _____
   _____

9. What licenses are available for cosmetologists? _____
   _____
   _____

10. Where do cosmetologists work? _____
    _____
    _____

Client Records

Activity E
Chapter 12

Name _____

Date _____ Period _____

When working with clients and customers, keeping accurate, up-to-date records is vital to effectively provide needed services. For this activity, respond to the following questions about documenting client information.

1. What contact information should be recorded about a client? _____
_____
_____

2. What basic information should a cosmetologist record about a client? _____
_____
_____
_____

3. What basic information should a home health aide record about a client? _____
_____
_____
_____

4. In what jobs would you need to know medical information about a client? _____
_____
_____

5. In what ways can documentation be done manually as well as electronically? _____
_____
_____

6. Why is it important to keep good and accurate records, as well as to keep clients' records confidential?
_____
_____
_____
_____
_____
_____
_____

Using Technology to Promote Personal Care Services

Activity F Name _____

Chapter 12 Date _____ Period _____

Many businesses use websites and other social media to promote the personal care services they offer. For this activity, look online and find a website for a hair salon near you. Respond to the following questions.

1. What is the name of the salon? _____

2. Where is the salon located? _____

3. What information is available on the website? _____
_____
_____
_____

4. Does the salon use other types of social media to promote their services? If so, what do they use?
_____

5. Does the website identify prices for services? If so, what are they? _____
_____
_____

6. What features of the website do you think are the most helpful for customers? _____
_____
_____

7. What features of the website do you think are the least helpful for customers? _____
_____
_____

8. Is there other information you would want to include on the website? If so, what would you add, and why?
_____
_____

9. Do you think the salon does a good job of promoting their services? Why or why not? _____
_____
_____

10. Based on the website, would you visit this salon? Why or why not? _____
_____
_____

Understanding Changes in Older Adulthood

Activity G
Chapter 12

Name _____

Date _____ Period _____

Physical, cognitive, and social changes taking place during older adulthood cause people to "slow down." Understanding the changes that occur during older adulthood is crucial to be able to effectively meet older adults' needs. For this activity, respond to the following statements and questions about changes that commonly occur during older adulthood.

1. Describe physical changes that commonly occur in older adulthood. _____
   _____
   _____

2. List three sensory changes that often occur during older adulthood. _____
   _____
   _____

3. Define *presbyopia*. _____
   _____
   _____

4. Define *tinnitus*. _____
   _____
   _____

5. Describe nutritional changes that can occur in older adulthood. _____
   _____
   _____

6. Explain how aging affects brain processing in older adulthood. _____
   _____
   _____

7. Explain why depression is often common in older adults. _____
   _____
   _____

8. Differentiate between *dementia* and *Alzheimer's disease*. _____
   _____
   _____
   _____

Chapter 13: Entrepreneurial Careers in Human Services

Defining Entrepreneurship

Activity A
Chapter 13

Name _____
Date _____ Period _____

Unscramble the letters to identify terms related to entrepreneurship. Give a definition for each term in the space provided.

1. PORTONAROCI _____
   _____
   _____

2. FILE HICCANGO _____
   _____
   _____

3. REALEERSFNC _____
   _____
   _____

4. GATETOC DUSTYRIN _____
   _____
   _____

5. PRERENTURNEE _____
   _____
   _____

6. TMDILIE BYILILAIT PCANOMY _____
   _____
   _____

7. TWOS SLYASINA _____
   _____
   _____

(Continued)

8. S PORTCOINOAR

9. TAKERM SLYASINA

10. LEOS TROPSHIPPROEIR

11. NERPHIPTARS

12. TRACTONSCOR

13. GETTAR TAKERM

14. SINBUSES SICLEEN

15. VOTECOPRAIE

16. SINBUSES LAPN

17. PETCOMEVIIT SLYASINA

18. ECVEUTIXE MARMUSY

Statements About Entrepreneurs

Activity B
Chapter 13

Name _____

Date _____ Period _____

Indicate whether you agree or disagree with the following statements about entrepreneurs. Then complete the sentence below.

Agree   **Disagree**

_____   _____   1. There are many human services careers that have entrepreneurship opportunities.

_____   _____   2. As an entrepreneur I am ready to assume all the responsibility for my business.

_____   _____   3. I believe that entrepreneurs have it easy and do not have a lot of work to do.

_____   _____   4. An entrepreneur is any person who starts and runs his or her own business.

_____   _____   5. I would be interested in being a freelancer or contractor.

_____   _____   6. Companies can benefit from using freelancers and contractors.

_____   _____   7. As an entrepreneur, I am ready to assume all the risks for my business.

_____   _____   8. Entrepreneurs have to follow a set schedule.

_____   _____   9. Most entrepreneurs make a huge profit their first year.

_____   _____   10. Working with young children would be fun.

_____   _____   11. I would like to work from home.

_____   _____   12. I would like to share office space with someone.

_____   _____   13. I wish to work outside instead of inside.

_____   _____   14. I wish to work inside instead of outside.

_____   _____   15. I want to work inside someone else's home.

I strongly (☐ agree / ☐ disagree) with statement _____ because _____

_____

_____

_____

_____

_____

_____

_____

Star Abilities

Activity C

Chapter 13

Name _____

Date _____ Period _____

Most entrepreneurs have a set of skills making it easier for them to be successful in running their business. For each star, identify a skill or ability and write it on the line below the star. Include an example of how this skill or ability is used as an entrepreneur.

110 *Principles of Human Services* Workbook

SWOT Analysis of a Business

Activity D
Chapter 13

Name _____

Date _____ Period _____

In the following table, fill out a SWOT Analysis for two businesses you are interested in starting. Your text gives valuable information on what you need to analyze a business. Remember to include strengths, weaknesses, opportunities, and threats for each one.

SWOT	Business 1	Business 2
Strengths		
Weaknesses		
Opportunities		
Threats		

1. Using the information from the analysis, which business would you like to start? Why?

   _____
   _____
   _____

2. What could you do to make your business stand out from other businesses doing the same thing in your town?

   _____
   _____
   _____

Ownership Advantages and Disadvantages

Activity E
Chapter 13

Name _____

Date _____ Period _____

Your textbook discusses six types of ownership that entrepreneurs can use for their business. Using your textbook and online resources, identify the six types of ownership and then list advantages and disadvantages of each.

Type of Ownership	Advantages	Disadvantages
Sole proprietorship		
Partnership		
Corporation		
S Corporation		
Limited liability company (LLC)		
Cooperative		

Parts of a Business Plan

Activity F
Chapter 13

Name _____

Date _____ Period _____

A business plan outlines the decisions and guidelines for a business. Using Figure 13.13 from the textbook as a guideline, answer the following questions.

1. What kind of business would you like to have? _____
   _____

2. What will sell in your community? _____
   _____

3. What is a mission statement? _____
   _____

4. What would your mission statement be? _____
   _____
   _____

5. What three objectives would you like to achieve with your business? _____
   _____
   _____
   _____
   _____
   _____

6. To whom would you market your business? _____
   _____

7. In what type of industry are you opening your business? Is it a growing industry? _____
   _____
   _____

8. What factors will make your company succeed? _____
   _____
   _____
   _____
   _____

(Continued)

9. What background experience, skills, and strengths do you personally bring to your new business?
_____
_____
_____
_____
_____

10. What type of ownership will you have? _____
_____

   Why have you selected this form? _____
_____
_____
_____
_____

11. What will your products or services be like? (Describe in detail.) _____
_____
_____
_____
_____
_____

12. How will you market your products or services? _____
_____
_____
_____
_____
_____

13. What is the pricing, fee, or leasing structure for your products or services? _____
_____
_____
_____
_____
_____

Chapter 14: Food and Nutrition Related Human Services

Career Match Up

Activity A

Chapter 14

Name _____

Date _____ Period _____

There are many career opportunities for human services workers in the fields of food and nutrition. For this activity, match each career description to its proper career.

Career Descriptions

_____ 1. Takes food and drink orders and serves items to customers.

_____ 2. Plans food programs in institutions, such as schools, cafeterias, hospitals, and prisons.

_____ 3. Provides nutrition information to students and foodservice workers in both public and private education, from child care centers through universities.

_____ 4. Oversees kitchen personnel and the food served in a restaurant or other facility.

_____ 5. Provides food and beverages for special occasions, one-time or infrequent events, or regularly scheduled functions.

_____ 6. Directs and coordinates the operations of services that prepare and serve food.

_____ 7. Assesses patients' needs and plans dietetic therapy to improve health through nutrition.

_____ 8. Performs the administrative duties and provides general business oversight in a foodservice establishment.

_____ 9. Works under the supervision of a RDN to provide health and nutrition care.

_____ 10. Deals with the everyday running of a foodservice establishment and often works on the dining floor.

_____ 11. Develops new products and determines whether food products are healthy, safe, palatable, and convenient.

Careers

A. assistant manager
B. caterer
C. clinical dietitian or nutritionist
D. executive chef
E. food and beverage serving worker
F. food scientist
G. foodservice manager
H. general manager
I. management dietitian
J. nutrition educator
K. registered dietetic technician

Establishing a Healthy Eating Style

Activity B
Chapter 14

Name _____

Date _____ Period _____

Establishing a healthy eating style early in life can help promote wellness. Healthful eating patterns established at a young age are also likely to continue throughout adulthood. For this activity, access the MyPlate website and follow the directions in each of the following parts.

Part 1

To complete this section, visit the home page of the MyPlate website. Then, locate the Everything You Eat and Drink Matters section under the Healthy Eating Style tab. Use this information to fill in the following table.

Food Groups	Nutrients	Health Benefits
Fruits		
Vegetables		
Grains		
Protein foods (lean or low fat)		
Dairy		

(Continued)

Name _____

Part 2

To build your healthy eating style, you need to know the amount of foods you need from each of the food groups. From the MyPlate website home page, locate the Daily Checklist feature under the Online Tools tab. Follow the directions on the website to create your Daily Checklist, which is a personalized food plan based on your age, sex, height, weight, and physical activity level. Using the results of your plan, answer the following questions.

1. How many total calories do I need each day? _____

2. How many cups of fruits should I have each day? _____

3. What types of fruits should I focus on? _____
_____
_____

4. How many cups of vegetables should I have each day? _____

5. What types of vegetables should I choose? _____
_____
_____

6. How many ounces of grains should I have each day? _____

7. What should half of my grain choices include? _____

8. How can I find out which foods are whole grains? _____
_____
_____

9. How many ounces of protein should I have each day? _____

10. In addition to lean meats and poultry, what other types of protein foods can I use to vary my protein routine?
_____
_____
_____

11. How many cups of dairy should I have each day? _____

12. Which dairy products should I choose to cut back on saturated fat? _____
_____
_____

13. What do I need to limit my sodium to each day? _____

14. What do I need to limit my saturated fat to each day? _____

15. What do I need to limit my added sugars to each day? _____

16. How much activity should I be getting each day? _____

(Continued)

Part 3

Choosing a variety of foods, and in the correct amounts, from each food group is essential to establishing a healthy eating style. Using your Daily Checklist from Part 2, fill in the amounts you need from each of the food groups in the second column of the following table. Then, identify the foods you would choose to meet your nutrient needs for a day and list these in the third column. Try to follow your plan for a day. As you go through the day, record the actual amounts and foods you eat in the fourth column. Compare these two columns. What changes would you consider making to create an eating style that can improve your health now and in the future?

Food Groups	Food Group Targets	Food Choices	Foods Eaten
Fruits	I need _____ cups 1 cup of fruit counts as • 1 cup raw or cooked fruit • ½ cup dried fruit • 1 cup 100% fruit juice		
Vegetables	I need _____ cups 1 cup vegetables counts as • 1 cup raw or cooked vegetables • 2 cups leafy salad greens • 1 cup 100% vegetable juice		
Grains	I need _____ ounce equivalents 1 ounce of grains counts as • 1 slice bread • 1 ounce ready-to-eat cereal • ½ cup cooked rice, pasta, or cereal		
Protein foods	I need _____ ounce equivalents 1 ounce of protein counts as • 1 ounce lean meat, poultry, or seafood • 1 egg • 1 Tbsp. peanut butter • ¼ cup cooked beans or peas • ½ ounce nuts or seeds		
Dairy	I need _____ cups 1 cup dairy counts as • 1 cup milk • 1 cup yogurt • 1 cup fortified soy beverage • 1½ ounces natural cheese or 2 ounces processed cheese		

Comparing Nutritional Needs

Activity C
Chapter 14

Name _____
Date _____ Period _____

No matter where you are in the lifespan, you have to eat. Use information from text pages 399–409 and the MyPlate website to compare and contrast the nutritional needs across the life cycle. Record your notes for each stage in the spaces provided.

Before and During Pregnancy	Infancy

The Toddler Years	Early Childhood

Middle Childhood	Adolescence

(Continued)

Early Adulthood	Middle Adulthood

Older Adulthood	Special Dietary Needs

Fad Diets—Myth or Truth?

Activity D Name _____

Chapter 14 Date _____ Period _____

Fad diets are diets promising quick and easy weight loss. You hear the hype about fad diets and how they are the latest thing. For this activity, conduct Internet research to investigate four current fad diets. Record your findings in the spaces provided. Be sure to cite your online sources. Share your findings with the rest of the class.

Fad Diet #1

Name of fad diet: _____

Company or person that originated the diet: _____
_____

Diet promises: _____
_____

Description of diet: _____
_____
_____
_____

Your opinion: _____
_____
_____

Online source: _____

Fad Diet #2

Name of fad diet: _____

Company or person that originated the diet: _____
_____

Diet promises: _____
_____

Description of diet: _____
_____
_____
_____

(Continued)

Your opinion: _____
_____
_____

Online source: _____

Fad Diet #3

Name of fad diet: _____

Company or person that originated the diet: _____
_____

Diet promises: _____
_____

Description of diet: _____
_____
_____
_____

Your opinion: _____
_____
_____

Online source: _____

Fad Diet #4

Name of fad diet: _____

Company or person that originated the diet: _____
_____

Diet promises: _____
_____

Description of diet: _____
_____
_____
_____

Your opinion: _____
_____
_____

Online source: _____

Understanding Recipes

Activity E Name _____

Chapter 14 Date _____ Period _____

The successful preparation of a meal or snack involves the ability to read and follow a recipe. This is why it is best to read through a whole recipe before beginning food preparation. For this activity, read the recipe below and then answer the questions that follow.

Recipe for Chicken Stir Fry

Yield: 4 servings

Ingredients
1 lb. boneless, skinless chicken breasts, slightly frozen
1 red pepper
¼ tsp. ginger, ground
2 Tbsp. soy sauce
1 Tbsp. cornstarch
⅔ c. cold water
2 Tbsp. sesame or vegetable oil
1 12-oz. bag broccoli florets, frozen
3 c. brown rice, cooked

Directions:
1. Slice chicken breast into thin slices.
2. Using a different knife and cutting board, wash red pepper then remove stem and seeds. Slice into thin strips.
3. Combine ginger, soy sauce, cornstarch, and water in a small bowl.
4. Preheat a wok or large skillet over medium high heat.
5. Carefully add 1 Tbsp. plus 2 tsp. of oil to wok or skillet. Add chicken and cook until chicken is lightly browned, stirring constantly. Remove chicken from wok and hold in warm oven.
6. Add remaining 1 tsp. oil to wok. Add red pepper and broccoli stirring constantly for 2 to 3 minutes.
7. Add chicken back into wok with vegetables.
8. Add mixture from step 3 to chicken and vegetables. Bring to a boil and cook until mixture thickens slightly.
9. Serve over hot rice.

---

1. After reading the recipe, are there any terms with which you are unfamiliar? If so, what are they? What do they mean?

_____
_____
_____
_____
_____

(Continued)

2. What five different abbreviations are used in this recipe? What units of measure do these abbreviations stand for?

      Abbreviations   **Units of Measure**

  _____   _____

  _____   _____

  _____   _____

  _____   _____

  _____   _____

3. How many servings does this recipe yield? _____

4. What equipment is needed to make this recipe? _____

_____

_____

5. Why is a different knife and cutting board needed to cut the red pepper? _____

_____

6. How much oil is needed to cook the chicken in the wok? _____

7. Which ingredients are added to the chicken and vegetables in step 8? _____

_____

8. How long does the red pepper and broccoli need to cook? _____

9. After cooking the chicken until lightly browned, what do you do with it? Why would you do this?

_____

_____

_____

10. How and when do you prepare the rice for this recipe? _____

_____

_____

_____

Chapter 15: Clothing Related Human Services

An Informational Interview

Activity A
Chapter 15

Name _____

Date _____ Period _____

Review the examples of clothing related human services career opportunities in Figure 15.1 of the textbook. Select the career area that interests you the most. Then, set up an informational interview with a professional in this career. Remember, when conducting an informational interview, come prepared and dress appropriately. Don't forget to send a thank-you message when you are done. The following questions will help you get started.

1. What is your job title? _____

2. How would you describe your typical day? _____
   _____
   _____
   _____
   _____
   _____

3. What variations occur in your set routine? _____
   _____
   _____
   _____

4. What do you like (and dislike) about your job? _____
   _____
   _____
   _____
   _____
   _____

5. How would you describe the work environment? _____
   _____
   _____

(Continued)

6. How did you get into this career field? _____
   _____
   _____

7. What skills are needed for this job? _____
   _____
   _____
   _____

8. What education and training is needed for this job? _____
   _____
   _____
   _____

9. What personal qualities do you feel are necessary to do your job effectively? _____
   _____
   _____
   _____

10. What are some examples of problems you have had to solve on the job? How did you solve them?
    _____
    _____
    _____
    _____
    _____

11. What are some examples of how fashion trends have caused you to apply new ideas and concepts on the job?
    _____
    _____
    _____
    _____

12. What are the rewards of this job? _____
    _____
    _____
    _____

(Continued)

Name _____

13. What are the demands of this job? _____
_____
_____
_____

14. If you could change anything about your job, what would it be? _____
_____
_____

15. What other professionals do you frequently interact with in this position? _____
_____
_____

16. What are the opportunities for career advancement? _____
_____
_____

17. Which courses do you feel are absolutely necessary to succeed in this job? _____
_____
_____

18. What activities, internships, or volunteer experiences would you recommend? ___
_____
_____

19. How do you keep up with the current trends in this field? _____
_____
_____

20. What advice do you have for me as a student? _____
_____
_____
_____

Other questions/responses: _____
_____
_____
_____

Fashion Forecast—Trend or Bust?

Activity B
Chapter 15

Name _____

Date _____ Period _____

Fashion forecasters predict what the upcoming trends will be. They predict what colors, fabrics, styles, and accessories will be bought by consumers the next year. For this activity, imagine you are a fashion forecaster for a major clothing store. Conduct online research to find out what is currently trending in women's and men's clothing. Report your findings in the following table and share them with the rest of the class.

Trends in Women's Clothing	Trends in Men's Clothing

Clothing Needs Across the Life Cycle

Activity C
Chapter 15

Name _____

Date _____ Period _____

As individuals change throughout the lifespan, so will their clothing needs. By understanding clothing needs at different stages of the life cycle, people's basic need for clothing can be met. In the table below, describe people's clothing needs during the various stages of the life cycle.

Stage	Description of Clothing Needs
Infants	
Toddlers	
Preschoolers	
School-age children	
Adolescents	
Young adults	
Middle-aged adults	
Older adults	
People with special needs	

Laundry Signs Identification

Activity D
Chapter 15

Name _____
Date _____ Period _____

Everyone needs to know how to properly care for their clothing. There are over 25 clothing care symbols found on clothing. Below are some of the most common ones. Identify the meaning of each of the following clothing care symbols. Check your responses with Figure 15.17 in the textbook.

1. _____

2. _____

3. _____

4. _____

5. _____

6. _____

7. _____

8. _____

9. _____

10. _____

11. _____

12. _____

13. _____

14. _____

15. _____

16. _____

17. _____

18. _____

19. _____

20. _____

130 *Principles of Human Services* Workbook

Identifying Construction Tools

Activity E
Chapter 15

Name _____
Date _____ Period _____

To construct individual clothing items, common tools people use consist of measuring, marking, cutting, and sewing tools. Therefore, it is important to be able to recognize these tools. In the spaces below each of the following pictures, write the name of the tool shown and identify whether it is a measuring, marking, cutting, or sewing tool.

1. Name: _____
   Type: _____

2. Name: _____
   Type: _____

3. Name: _____
   Type: _____

4. Name: _____
   Type: _____

5. Name: _____
   Type: _____

6. Name: _____
   Type: _____

(Continued)

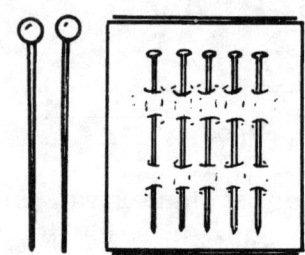 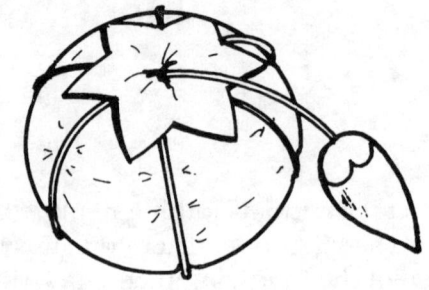

7. Name:_____   8. Name:_____

   Type:_____   Type:_____

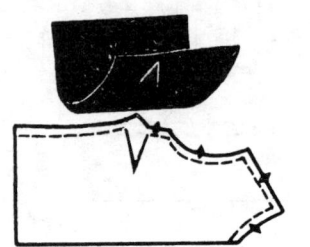 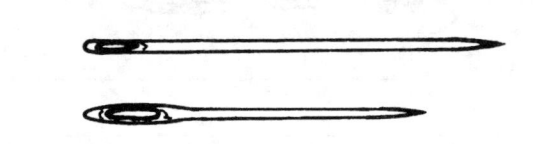

9. Name:_____   10. Name:_____

   Type:_____   Type:_____

 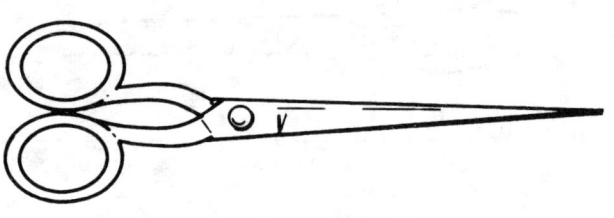

11. Name:_____   12. Name:_____

    Type:_____   Type:_____

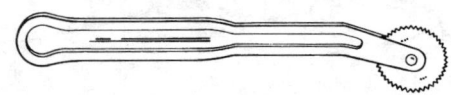

13. Name:_____   14. Name:_____

    Type:_____   Type:_____

Making Simple Repairs and Alterations

Activity F
Chapter 15

Name _____
Date _____ Period _____

There are many reasons to repair and alter your clothing. Knowing how to make simple repairs and alterations to clothing you already own can save you from costly professional repairs or replacements. For this activity, put the steps for each repair or alteration into the correct order.

Replacing a Button

_____ 1. Bring the needle and thread to the back of the fabric and knot the thread. Repeat the knot for extra security. Then cut the thread.

_____ 2. Put a toothpick between the fabric and button, centered between the two buttonholes. Bring the needle up through the fabric and button. Bring the thread over the toothpick and back down through the button.

_____ 3. Thread a hand sewing needle and secure the thread ends with a knot.

_____ 4. For a button with four holes, use the same steps as for one with two holes.

_____ 5. Repeat the stitch to make six stitches over the button. Too many stitches can weaken or tear the fabric.

_____ 6. Mark the spot where the button should be located. To do this, start at the back of the fabric and bring the needle up to the front and through one buttonhole. Bring threaded needle down through the other buttonhole.

_____ 7. Remove toothpick. Pull the button up and bring the needle between the fabric and button. Make a shank by winding thread around stitches several times. This will add space between the button and fabric, which makes the button stay on longer and also makes buttoning easier.

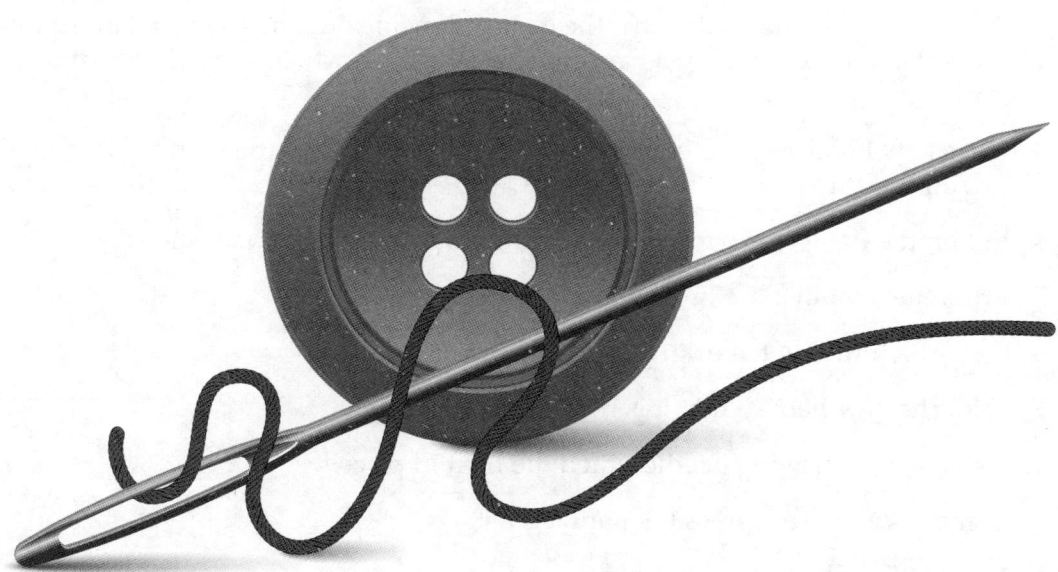

mylisa/Shutterstock.com

(Continued)

Repairing a Torn Seam

_____ 1. Thread a hand sewing needle and secure the thread ends with a knot.

_____ 2. Repeat stitching along the length of the rip or tear. Allow some overlap with the unbroken seam on each end of the repair to give a smoother and more secure finish.

_____ 3. If possible, press the seam together flat to prevent bunching when sewn.

_____ 4. Sew several small stitches in the same place on the fabric. Pull the thread and cut the end as close to the fabric as possible.

_____ 5. Bring the threaded needle through the seam just below the rip or tear. Push the needle through to the other side of the seam.

_____ 6. Turn the garment inside out and examine the seam.

Patching a Hole

_____ 1. Cut the patch to cover the hole plus extend beyond at least ¼ inch on all sides.

_____ 2. Machine sew or hand sew to reinforce, if desired.

_____ 3. Using fusible web, adhere the patch in place using a hot iron following product instructions.

_____ 4. Check if the hole or rip can be repaired by incorporating it into a seam and following the seam repair instructions. Make sure that doing so does not result in pulling, puckering, or changing the fit of the garment.

_____ 5. If the hole or rip needs to be covered with a patch, choose a compatible fabric to use to make the patch. The fabric can match in color or act as a decorative contrast.

Shortening Length on Pants

_____ 1. While standing straight in front of a full-length mirror, have a friend or assistant pin the hem in place.

_____ 2. After removing the pants, turn the garment inside out and place on an ironing board. Press the new hemline up as indicated by the pins, which should be removed as the hem is pressed.

_____ 3. Once new hemline is determined, finish the raw edge of the hem by stitching with a sewing machine.

_____ 4. Put on the pants, securing fasteners, and donning appropriate shoes.

_____ 5. Press the hem in place once again.

_____ 6. Carefully pull out the original hem thread.

_____ 7. Trim the new hem so that it is not too wide.

_____ 8. Using a hand sewing needle, stitch the hem in place.

_____ 9. Using a steam iron, press the pant leg flat.

_____ 10. Carefully pull out the original hem thread.

Chapter 16: Housing Related Human Services

Housing Related Career Research

Activity A
Chapter 16

Name _____
Date _____ Period _____

There are many career opportunities for people interested in working with housing, whether that housing is long-term or short-term. For this activity, refer to your textbook and the OOH to summarize what each of the following professionals do.

1. Housing specialists: _____
   _____
   _____

2. Real estate brokers and sales agents: _____
   _____
   _____

3. Property managers: _____
   _____
   _____
   _____

4. Home furnishings sales and marketing staff: _____
   _____
   _____
   _____

5. Residential interior designers: _____
   _____
   _____
   _____

6. Commercial interior designers: _____
   _____
   _____
   _____

An Informational Interview

Activity B
Chapter 16

Name _____

Date _____ Period _____

Choose the career area from Activity A that interests you the most. Then, set up an informational interview with a professional in this career. The following questions will help you get started.

1. What is your job title? _____

2. How would you describe your typical day? _____
_____
_____
_____
_____
_____

3. What variations occur in your set routine? _____
_____
_____
_____
_____

4. What do you like (and dislike) about your job? _____
_____
_____
_____
_____
_____

5. How would you describe the work environment? _____
_____
_____
_____

6. How did you get into this career field? _____
_____
_____

Name _____

7. What skills are needed for this job? _____
_____
_____
_____

8. What education and training is needed for this job? _____
_____
_____
_____

9. What personal qualities do you feel are necessary to do your job effectively? _____
_____
_____
_____

10. What are some examples of problems you have had to solve on the job? How did you solve them?
_____
_____
_____
_____
_____
_____
_____

11. What are some examples of the most popular design trends? _____
_____
_____

12. What are the rewards of this job? _____
_____
_____
_____

13. What are the demands of this job? _____
_____
_____
_____

14. If you could change anything about your job, what would it be? _____
_____
_____

15. What other professionals do you frequently interact with in this position? _____
_____
_____

16. What are the opportunities for career advancement?_____
_____
_____

17. Which courses do you feel are absolutely necessary to succeed in this job? _____
_____
_____

18. What activities, internships, or volunteer experiences would you recommend? _____
_____
_____
_____

19. How do you keep up with the current trends in this field?_____
_____
_____

20. What advice do you have for me as a student?_____
_____
_____
_____

Other questions/responses:_____
_____
_____
_____
_____
_____
_____

Changing Housing Needs

Activity C
Chapter 16

Name _____

Date _____ Period _____

Arrange to interview an older adult to find out how his or her housing needs have changed over the lifespan. You can begin the interview with the following questions, but add questions of your own, too.

1. Where was the first place you ever lived independently of your parents? _____
_____

2. In what ways did this housing meet your needs? _____
_____
_____

3. What did you especially like and dislike about this housing? _____
_____
_____

4. When did you move from this housing, and where did you relocate? What caused your housing needs to change?
_____
_____
_____

5. How many other times have you moved, and where did you relocate each time? Why did you decide to move when you did?
_____
_____
_____

6. Do you think you will ever move again? Why or why not? _____
_____

7. What special design features does your current housing have to help you meet your physical needs? (e.g., ramps, handrails, wide hallways)
_____
_____

8. Other questions/comments: _____
_____
_____
_____

Understanding Universal Design

Activity D
Chapter 16

Name _____

Date _____ Period _____

During any stage of life, accessibility is important. Sometimes special circumstances, such as an accident or special need, warrant consideration. For this activity, research universal design guidelines, principles, and applications that you could apply in developing an overall design to meet your clients' special design needs. Share your ideas with the rest of the class.

Scenario 1: *Josh and Megan live in a two-story home. Recently, Megan has been losing her balance and falling a lot. She went to the doctor and has been diagnosed with multiple sclerosis. Josh and Megan have hired you to make their two-story house safe for Megan. What would you recommend?*

_____
_____
_____
_____
_____
_____
_____

Scenario 2: *Charles is a 68-year-old widow living on his own in a one-bedroom apartment. His eyesight is failing and he is having more difficulty navigating his way through his home. What would you recommend?*

_____
_____
_____
_____
_____
_____

Scenario 3: *Jakeel and Aisha recently moved into her grandparents' old house. Jakeel and Aisha love to cook together, but this new kitchen is not accommodating for their varying heights. They would like you to redesign the kitchen so it is functional for both of them. What would you do?*

_____
_____
_____
_____
_____
_____

Creating a Cleaning and Maintenance Schedule

Activity E　　　　　　　　　　　Name _____

Chapter 16　　　　　　　　　　　Date _____ Period _____

Creating a cleaning and maintenance schedule can help you keep track of when tasks need to be done around the home, and by whom. For this activity, develop a cleaning schedule for your family's home using the template below.

Task	Time Period	Person Responsible

Using the Elements of Design

Activity F
Chapter 16

Name _____

Date _____ Period _____

Designers use each of the elements of design as they alter, modify, and create visually pleasing interiors for their clients. For this activity, indicate whether the following statements are true or false. If the statement is false, rewrite the underlined portion to make the statement true.

_____ 1. The elements of design include line, shape, form, <u>harmony, balance, pattern,</u> color, and light. _____

_____ 2. <u>Shape</u> is the most basic element of design. _____

_____ 3. When a two-dimensional shape becomes three dimensional, it becomes a <u>geometric shape</u>. _____

_____ 4. <u>Proxemics</u> is the study of how people create the space around them. _____

_____ 5. <u>Texture</u> is the feel or appearance of a surface. _____

_____ 6. <u>Line</u>, which is often used with texture, is the orderly repetition of a specific design. _____

_____ 7. Horizontal lines in a design give a feeling of <u>calm</u>. _____

_____ 8. <u>Texture</u> can make a room appear brighter. _____

_____ 9. The primary colors are <u>blue, red, and green</u>. _____

_____ 10. To create <u>tints</u>, add black to the hue. _____

_____ 11. Red, yellow, and orange are all examples of <u>warm colors</u>. _____

_____ 12. A <u>triad color scheme</u> is created by taking one hue and changing the intensity and value. _____

_____ 13. Complementary color schemes utilize variants of hues that are <u>opposite each other</u> on the color wheel. _____

_____ 14. <u>Value</u> is the lightness or darkness of a color that is produced by adding white or black. _____

_____ 15. Orange, purple, and green are examples of <u>tertiary colors</u>. _____

_____ 16. Cool colors tend to be <u>calming, stable, or relaxing</u>. _____

The Principles of Design

Activity G
Chapter 16

Name _____

Date _____ Period _____

The principles of design are the guidelines for effectively using the elements of design. Utilizing the principles of design creates pleasing and interesting compositions or spaces. For this activity, identify and describe each of the principles of design and give an example of its use in an interior design.

Principles of Design	Example 1	Example 2
Harmony		
Emphasis		
Rhythm		
Balance		
Proportion		

Housing Related Terms Review

Activity H
Chapter 16

Name _____

Date _____ Period _____

Test your match-making skills by matching the housing related terms with the correct definitions.

Definitions

_____ 1. Lightness or darkness of a color that is produced by adding white or black.

_____ 2. Housing for older adults who can care for themselves, but desire the community support of those of similar age.

_____ 3. Process of shaping the experience of interior space through the manipulation of space, the application of the elements and principles of design, and the use of materials.

_____ 4. Darker values created by adding black to the hue.

_____ 5. Harmony, emphasis, rhythm, balance, and proportion.

_____ 6. Colors.

_____ 7. Environments for older adults that provide gradually expanded oversight and help with daily activities.

_____ 8. Universal standard for determining size and scale of a design.

_____ 9. Special housing for older adults that offers more intense nursing care, usually provided by medical staff.

_____ 10. Something that attracts the eye.

_____ 11. Combinations of different colors in various tints, shades, and intensities.

_____ 12. Colors created by adding grey, which lowers the intensity of the colors.

_____ 13. Diagram that shows the relationships between primary, secondary, and tertiary colors.

_____ 14. Housing design that meets the physical needs of people of all ages and abilities.

_____ 15. Line, shape, form, space, texture, pattern, color, and light.

_____ 16. Study of how people create the space around them.

_____ 17. Lighter values created by adding white to the hue.

Terms

A. assisted living housing
B. color schemes
C. color wheel
D. commercial interior designer
E. elements of design
F. focal point
G. hues
H. human scale
I. independent living communities
J. interior design
K. nursing homes
L. principles of design
M. proxemics
N residential interior designer
O. shades
P. tints
Q. tones
R. universal design
S. value